LUFTWAFFE FIGHTER UNITS
MEDITERRANEAN 1941-44

BY CHRISTOPHER SHORES

COLOUR PLATES BY
JERRY SCUTTS
MICHAEL ROFFE
RICHARD HOOK

OSPREY PUBLISHING LONDON

Published in 1978 by
Osprey Publishing Ltd
Member company of the George Philip Group
12–14 Long Acre, London WC2E 9LP
© Copyright 1978 Osprey Publishing Ltd

ISBN 0 85045 294 5

Unless otherwise credited, all photographs are courtesy of
Bundesarchiv, Koblenz.

Filmset by BAS Printers Limited, Over Wallop,
Hampshire, England
Printed in Hong Kong

MOVE TO THE DESERT

At the start of 1941 it had become abundantly clear to Hitler that he would have to provide some aid for his Italian ally Mussolini, whose dreams of a Mediterranean empire were in danger of being shattered beyond repair, and it fell to the Luftwaffe to supply the first such assistance. During the previous October, the Italians had invaded northwestern Greece, expecting a swift conquest. Instead the Greeks had resisted with spirit, counterattacking and driving the invaders back across the border into Albania (annexed by Italy in 1938). By the beginning of 1941, units of the Royal Air Force were present in Greece, raising the possibility of a major British thrust into the Balkans generally. This could prove a most dangerous threat to German plans for the forthcoming invasion of Russia, which at that time was envisaged to commence in the late spring. In December 1940 a reconnaissance in force across the Egyptian frontier by a small British force had turned into a full-scale offensive after achieving unexpectedly large initial gains. It was now rolling the Italian army back across Libya at a frightening rate, threatening to drive it from North Africa altogether.

Winter had slowed the pace of events in Greece, but the situation in Libya required speedy action. To support a presence in North Africa from the Italian mainland, it was necessary first to neutralize the British air and naval bases on the Mediterranean island of Malta, and indeed desirable to occupy them if possible. Consequently, in January 1941 units of the Luftwaffe, fresh from their activities over England during the previous autumn, were despatched from western Europe to Sicily: from there attacks were launched against the British Mediterranean Fleet, and against Malta itself. At the same time a small element was sent across to Tripoli, in western Libya, as a harbinger of a mixed expeditionary force.

At first the units arriving included medium and dive bomber, transport, army co-operation and

The first Luftwaffe fighters to reach the Mediterranean area were initially based in Sicily in early 1941. Here are a Messerschmitt Bf109E (foreground) of 7/JG 26, and a Bf110D of III/ZG 26. Interesting details include the yellow nose of the 109; white engine cowlings of the 110; the camouflaged upper forward portion of the 110's underwing auxiliary tanks; and the Heinkel He111s of KG 26 in the background.

reconnaissance, and *Zerstörer* formations, but no single-engined fighters. The *Zerstörer* aircraft were Messerschmitt Bf110s of *Major* Kaschka's III/ZG 26, which had been involved in fighting over France and England during 1940. They had left the Channel coast during December, and arrived at Treviso shortly afterwards. In January they flew on to Palermo in Sicily, where their duties included escorting transport aircraft and shipping crossing the sea to Africa, and escorting bombers attacking Malta and units of the British Fleet.

During mid-January 1941, a series of heavy air raids was made on Valetta's Grand Harbour, Malta, where the British aircraft carrier *Illustrious* had sought shelter after suffering severe damage during a Luftwaffe dive bomber attack. It was there that III/ZG 26 saw its first action in the area. First appearing over the island on 18 January, the unit was able to claim three of the defending Hurricanes shot down without loss on the 19th. Thereafter the raids tailed off, and no such further action followed. Later in the month, joined briefly by 2 *Staffel* from I/ZG 26, the unit moved much of its strength to airfields in the Tripoli area, making the initial sorties there during the middle of February. On the 19th of that month, Hurricanes were met again, two being shot down for one loss.

The presence of the *Zerstörer* in Sicily had been rendered less necessary by the arrival at Gela on 9 February of the first unit of Messerschmitt Bf109E fighters. This initial contingent was only small, comprising 7 *Staffel* of *Jagdgeschwader* 26 'Schlageter'. This unit of nine aircraft had been active throughout the Battle of Britain, and was led by a highly experienced pilot, *Oberleutnant* Joachim Müncheberg, who already had twenty-three victories to his credit, and had been awarded the *Ritterkreuz* (Knight's Cross to the Iron Cross) during the previous September. The Bf109s were swiftly committed to action over Malta, Müncheberg personally making his first claim against one of the defending Hurricanes three days after arrival. Throughout the next two months the *Staffel* regularly joined Italian fighters in escorting bombers over Malta, and in flying freelance fighter sweeps (*Freie Jagd*), the very capable German pilots taking a dreadful toll of the defending fighters. These latter were frequently flown by pilots fresh

Staffelkapitän **and most successful pilot of 7/JG 26 was** *Oblt.* **Joachim Müncheberg, seen here in the cockpit of his Bf109E on return to Sicily after a sortie over Malta. Points of interest include the radio mast pennant and the script 'S' badge of JG 26.**

from training units, or recently retrained from other flying duties.

As the spring approached, the planned invasion of Russia was put back to allow the diversion of forces necessary to clear up the situation in the Balkans, where in Yugoslavia King Peter had been forced to abdicate, and the Yugoslav participation in the Axis Tripartite Pact was revoked. This new departure, coupled with the increasing British presence in Greece, made the securing of the southern flank an absolute prerequisite of any operations in the east.

A two-pronged assault was proposed, one force striking from Austria into Yugoslavia, while a second would move through the Rupel Pass from Bulgaria into Greece. Strong elements of the Luftwaffe were to join the ground forces in a *Blitzkrieg*-style assault, and this time substantial fighter elements were involved. To support the main attack, *Stab*, and II and III *Gruppen* of *Maj.* Johannes Trautloft's JG 54 'Grunherz', together with I/JG 27, moved to the Graz area of Austria; *Gruppenkommandeurn* were respectively *Hauptmann* Dietrich Hrabak, Arnold Lignitz and Eduard Neumann, *Stab*/JG 27 under *Maj.* Wolfgang Schellmann, with II and III *Gruppen* (*Hptm.* Wolfgang Lippert and Max Dobislav), and I(J)/LG 2 (*Hptm.* Herbert Ihlefeld) under its command, moved to Belica and Vrba in Bulgaria, while *Maj.* Bernhard Woldenga's *Stab*/JG 77 with II *Gruppe* (*Hptm.*

Lange) and III *Gruppe* (*Maj*. Alexander von Winterfeldt) went to Deta, near Temesvar. At the same time *Maj*. Johann Schalk led *Stab*, and I (*Hptm*. Wilhelm Makrocki) and II/ZG 26 (*Hptm*. Ralph von Rettberg) to Sofia. III/JG 52 was held in reserve at Rumania's Bucharest-Pipera airfield under *Maj*. Gotthardt Handrick, where defence of the Ploesti oilfields and refineries could also be provided in case of any attack. Italian units were also to take part, while from Sicily 7/JG 26 and III/ZG 26 flew to southeastern Italy to attack targets in western Yugoslavia.

The attack was launched on 6 April 1941, armoured columns striking deep into Yugoslavia at once. Raids by the Luftwaffe on Belgrade and other centres brought up the Yugoslav interceptors in force, and the units of JG 54 quickly achieved considerable successes against Yugoslav Bf109E and IK-3 fighters. Next day II *Gruppe* cut a formation of Yugoslav Blenheim I bombers to pieces, whilst Hurricanes and IK-2 fighters were also added to the victory tallies; III *Gruppe* undertook a number of fighter-bomber (*Jabo*) sorties as well, while I/JG 27 carried out some ground strafing, but all opposition in the air was swiftly crushed. Flying from Taranto and Grottaglie, 7/JG 26 and III/ZG 26 also made a number of ground attacks, Müncheberg shooting down a single Yugoslav Fury biplane. The partici-

A Messerschmitt Bf110D coded 3U-DD of *Stab* III/ZG 26 in Sicily, 1941.

pation of the *Zerstörergruppe* in the campaign was brief however, for on the 7th it returned to Sicily, followed next day by the Bf109E *Staffel*. Two days later, I/JG 27 was ordered from Graz to southern Germany to prepare for a move to North Africa.

Meanwhile, from Bulgaria the Bf109E *Verbände* of *Fliegerkorps* VIII began operations over both northern Greece and Yugoslavia. Success was mixed: on the very first morning (6 April) *Leutnant* Fritz Geisshardt of I(J)/LG 2 shot down four Yugoslav Hawker Furies while *Unteroffizier* Steigleder of I/ZG 26 claimed a pair of Bf109Es, but in the afternoon, 8 *Staffel* from III/JG 27 was badly bounced by RAF Hurricanes of No. 33 Squadron while engaged in a *Jabo* mission down the Rupel Pass. At least four of the Bf109Es were lost, three pilots failing to return and one more being wounded.

From 10 April all activities were directed over Greece, where on the 13th, II/JG 27 was able to avenge its fellow *Gruppe* when 3 pilots from 6 *Staffel* engaged a formation of 6 British Blenheim IV bombers from No. 211 Squadron, shooting down every one. More combats followed over Greece, at least 8 British and Greek fighters (4 Gladiators, 3 PZL P-24s and 1 Hurricane) being claimed shot down on 15 April, 3 of them by *Oblt*. Gustav Rödel of II/JG 27. A squadron of Blenheims was wiped out on the ground at Niamata, and forty-four Yugoslav

Greek officers inspect a Bf109E of III/JG 77 which has come to grief during a strafing attack on an airfield in Greece, April 1941. (IWM)

minute battle, several aircraft of each side fell, amongst them a Hurricane flown by the most successful RAF pilot of the Greek campaign, Squadron Leader M. T. St J. Pattle, who is believed to have shot down something of the order of fifty Axis aircraft. The *Zerstörerflieger* returned to base having undoubtedly had the best of the battle, while other Hurricanes were claimed by Bf109 pilots of JG 27; twelve more Blenheims were strafed on the ground at Menidi.

With the airfields around Athens untenable, the British units withdrew to Argos in southern Greece, where Bf109s of JG 77 and Bf110s of ZG 26 found them on 23 April, the Germans claiming thirteen Hurricanes destroyed on the ground and one in the air. The victor of this latter combat was *Hptm.* Lange, *Kommandeur* of II/JG 77, who was in turn shot down and killed. It was virtually the end of the air war in Greece, all RAF formations withdrawing to Crete or Egypt. From 6 to 30 April Luftwaffe crews had claimed sixty-four RAF machines shot down and eighty-seven more destroyed on the

aircraft, which had escaped to the Greek airfield of Paramythia, were also destroyed. On that date however, *Ltn.* Hans-Jacob Arnoldy of II/JG 77, a veteran of the Norwegian campaign with seven victories to his credit, was shot down by an RAF Hurricane and crash-landed, dying of the wounds he suffered. A couple of days later, a complete Greek Gladiator squadron was strafed to destruction at Paramythia by the jubilant Messerschmitt pilots.

By the middle of April the centre of fighting in the air had moved south to the Athens area, culminating on the 20th in a big dog-fight between Bf110s of 5/ZG 26, which were escorting Ju87s, and fifteen intercepting Hurricanes. During a twenty

After brief service over Yugoslavia in April 1941, I/JG 27 was posted to Africa via Sicily, where this particular Bf109E was photographed.

In September 1941, II/JG 27 joined I *Gruppe* in Libya, equipped with the first Bf109Fs to serve in Africa. Here one of the unit's aircraft, carrying the 'Bear of Berlin' insignia on the nose, is seen sharing a dispersal with a Junkers Ju88A of LG 1.

ground. During the British withdrawal, *Jabo* of III/JG 77 attacked shipping off the coast of Greece, *Hptm*. Wolf-Dietrich Huy sinking a 20,000 ton troop transport in the Bay of Nauplion.

By the end of the month, the two *Gruppen* of JG 27, plus I(J)/LG 2 had arrived at Athens/Eleusis airfield, with II and III/JG 77 occupying Tanagra, and I and II/ZG 26 moving into Argos. With the cessation of hostilities however, some redispositions were made. During the April fighting, JG 54 had moved first to airfields in Rumania, and then to the Belgrade area. On 25 April the unit had handed its Bf109Es to JG 77 and withdrawn to Germany to re-equip with new Bf109Fs ready for the Russian invasion. The *Geschwader* had claimed eighteen victories over Yugoslavia for a single non-operational loss. The remaining elements of JG 27 now began to follow suit, III *Gruppe* moving to Sicily on 5 May, while II *Gruppe* left for the Reich on the 11th. To make good these departures, II/ZG 76, under *Hptm*. Erich Groth, arrived from northern Germany and joined ZG 26 at Argos.

For operations over Crete, JG 77, joined by I(J)/LG 2, moved to Molai in the south Peloponnese, from whence in mid-May all six *Gruppen* of fighters and *Zerstörer* began a series of concentrated attacks on the island's weak air defences. This began on the 14th, when 15 aircraft were claimed destroyed on the ground and 8 in the air, for the loss of 2 Bf109s and a single Bf110. The latter machine, shot down by the airfield ground defences, was flown by one

Newly arrived Bf109Es of I/JG 27 peel off over the Libyan desert, early 1941.

By late 1941, I/JG 27 had been re-equipped with Bf109Fs. An aircraft of this *Gruppe* undergoes undercarriage retraction tests with the engine running. Note the ground crew holding down the tail.

of the greatest *Zerstörer Experten, Oblt.* Sophus Baagoe of 5/ZG 26, victor of fourteen combats. Baagoe had been one of the successful pilots over Athens on the day Pattle was killed. He was later posthumously awarded the *Ritterkreuz*.

More attacks followed, the RAF component in Crete swiftly being rendered impotent. On 20 May large fleets of Ju52/3m transport aircraft took in a Luftwaffe paratroop force and air-landing units, while the defences were heavily bombed by He11s, Do17s and Ju87s, under an umbrella of fighters. The Bf109s and Bf110s undertook many ground attack sorties at this time, but losses to the concentrated gunfire of the defenders were heavy, JG 77 alone losing five pilots on the first day. One of them was *Oblt.* Helmut Henz of II/JG 77, the second *Kommandeur* to be lost by the *Gruppe* within a month. Indeed, so heavy were the losses to ground fire and to landing accidents on the poor Peloponnese airfields, that on 28 May III/JG 52 was sent from reserve in Rumania to strengthen

JG 77. Before the *Gruppe* could commence operation however, the fighting on Crete had ceased.

Meanwhile, substantial units of the British Mediterranean Fleet had appeared around Crete during late May, as efforts were made to prevent the passage of German reinforcements and heavy equipment to the island by sea. Numerous dive bombing attacks were carried out by Ju87s and Ju88s against these vessels, in which task they were aided to no small extent by the *Jabo*. On 22 May *Oblt.* Huy and *Oblt.* Kurt Ubben of III/JG 77 attacked HMS *Warspite*, succeeding in inflicting considerable damage by putting the battleship's starboard armament out of action. Later in the same day a lone Bf109E of I(J)/LG 2, returning from a fruitless search, spotted the cruiser *Fiji*, which was stationary. This vessel had been under attack all day but had escaped damage until now. The pilot dived steeply and placed his 250 kilogram bomb directly alongside, the explosion tearing a great hole in the ship below the waterline. He radioed for help, but by the time another aircraft from his unit had arrived and attacked, the vessel was already on the way down—the largest warship so far to be sunk by fighter-bomber attack.

As the fighting on Crete approached a climax, RAF aircraft began appearing again, having made the long flight from airfields in Egypt. On 25 May, *Hptm.* Ihlefeld and his wingman, *Ltn.* Geisshardt of I(J)/LG 2, were able to shoot down two Hurricanes; a further Hurricane was to be credited to Geisshardt during the period. Herbert Ihlefeld, one of the top scorers of 1940, had been shot down by ground fire during the fighting over Greece and had spent over a week as a prisoner.

With the end of hostilities on Crete, the Germans began redeploying for the now-delayed invasion of Russia, most units leaving the Mediterranean area forthwith. Early in June the *Gruppen* of JG 77 left for Vienna and Bucharest, while III/JG 52 flew back to Rumania; I and II/ZG 26 were transferred to Celle in north-western Germany, whilst II/ZG 76 (minus 4 *Staffel*) returned to the area of the German Bight. During the period of operations in the Balkans, *Jagd-* and *Zerstörerflieger* had claimed 167 Yugoslavian, British and Greek aircraft shot down, and 417 more destroyed on the ground. Amongst the more successful pilots were *Oblt.* Gustav Rödel of II/JG 27 and *Ltn.* Fritz Geisshardt of I(J)/LG 2, with six victories each. In JG 77, Erwin Clausen, Günther Hannak, and Emil Omert had each claimed three; 122 of the aircraft destroyed on the ground had been credited to I/ZG 26. On the debit side, 20 Bf109 pilots and 17 Bf110 crews had been killed, taken prisoner, or were otherwise reported missing.

One *Staffel* of ZG 76 had remained in the area for special duties; as soon as II/ZG 76 had arrived in Greece, 4 *Staffel* had been detached and sent to Iraq, its Bf110s freshly repainted with the national markings of that country, in order to assist in a rebellion against the British presence there. This was not to prove a happy chapter for the unit, for its base at Mosul was virtually unprotected and in the air the Germans faced Gladiator and Hurricane fighters of the RAF. In the face of continual strafing attacks on their base, the personnel were forced to withdraw just before the Iraqi collapse, leaving behind the wreckage of all their aircraft. Only one victory had been recorded—a Gladiator claimed by *Ltn.* Martin Drewes—while one crew had been lost in combat; it is believed that at least two Bf110s had actually been shot down.

SHIELD OVER ROMMEL

In Africa meanwhile III/ZG 26 had returned to Libya to take part in the initial operations planned by the newly arrived *General* Erwin Rommel. There the *Gruppe* was very active from early April, escorting Ju87s and strafing British airfields and other targets as Rommel's tentative probes developed into an assault which drove the critically weakened British back into Egypt. Throughout the month the unit was involved in frequent combats—mainly with Hurricanes and Blenheims—and while suffering several losses, was able to increase its score quite regularly. By mid-April the Bf110s, now frequently joined by Italian CR42 and G-50bis fighters, were much involved in raids on the bypassed port of Tobruk, where the garrison was holding out stubbornly. In this area they were about to be joined by a new arrival.

On 18 April 1941, the first Bf109E fighters arrived in Libya, operated by I/JG 27. It will be recalled that this *Gruppe* had played a short and relatively minor

Pilots of II/JG 27 prepare to *Alarmstart* their Bf109Fs from a desert airfield in early 1942.

part in the invasion of Yugoslavia, before being pulled back to southern Germany and on to Africa. The unit was not one of the best known in the Luftwaffe at this time, having claimed some 62 victories during the Battle of France, but only 32 more throughout the fighting over England during the previous summer. Led by *Hptm.* Eduard Neumann, who had 9 victories to his credit (2 of them claimed during the Spanish Civil War), the unit's most successful pilots were *Oblt.* Gerhard Homuth (15 victories), leader of 3 *Staffel, Oblt.* Ludwig Franzisket (14 victories), *Gruppenadjutant,* and *Oblt.* Karl-Heinz Redlich (10 victories), *Staffelkapitän* of 1 *Staffel.* Other successful pilots included *Ltn.* Willi Kothmann with 7 victories, *Oberfeldwebel* Hermann Förster with 6, and a young cadet, *Oberfähnrich* Hans-Joachim Marseille, with 7. The latter was a difficult character, always in trouble with his superiors; he was, however, to find his niche in the desert, and to elevate his unit into one of the most famous in the Luftwaffe.

After its recent moves from one end of Europe to the other, and then to Africa, the *Gruppe* was in some confusion, arriving in Libya with no proper tropical equipment or clothing, personnel being forced to buy what they could in Tripoli as they arrived. The unit was immediately rushed into action, appearing over the front on 19 April, the day after its arrival. Four Hurricanes were shot down for the loss of one Messerschmitt, which crash-landed. Two of these first victories went to Redlich and another to *Ltn.* Werner Schroer, the pilot who crash-landed. Like Marseille, Schroer was to become one of the big names of the African campaign. First, however, he would be shot down for a second time two days later.

I/JG 27 suffered its first casualty on 21 April, but was soon making its presence felt over Tobruk, where the position of the defending Hurricanes was swiftly made untenable. During a big engagement there on the 23rd, seven victories were claimed against Blenheims and Hurricanes, Redlich and Franzisket claiming two apiece. Another British aircraft became Marseille's first victory in Africa but he, like Schroer, was shot down and crash-landed. By the end of April, 14 victories had been claimed for the loss of 7 Bf109s and 3 pilots. May was to prove a quieter month however, as both sides,

The great desert *Experte, Ltn.* Hans-Joachim Marseille of I/JG 27. The rudder of his Bf109F indicates forty-eight victories, dating this photograph as mid-February 1942.

exhausted by their exertions, strove to build up their strength.

This lull allowed I/JG 27 time to acclimatize to the hard conditions of the desert—the blazing heat of the day; the sudden, unexpected cold of the night; the swirling dust that permeated everything, ruining food and reducing the lives of motors and guns; the ever-present swarms of flies; and of course the shortage of fresh water. Life was nevertheless healthy and a fine cameraderie soon began to build up as the men were thrown together and forced to rely on their own resources. Above all, the desert war was as clean as it was possible for war to be. There were no civilians to get hurt, little private property to be destroyed or expropriated, and the enemy was fair and chivalrous, allowing him to be treated with an almost friendly respect.

* * *

While I/JG 27 was recording its initial achievements in Africa, 7/JG 26 was continuing to make life very difficult for a substantially larger force of Hurricanes in Sicily. By the end of May the *Staffel* had claimed forty-two aerial victories, and had also made several strafing attacks on airfields, destroying more Hurricanes on the ground. It had also attacked the seaplane base at Kalafrana Bay a number of times, destroying two or three Sunderland flying boats there. It was the moral ascendency that the *Staffel* sustained over the defending fighters that was probably its greatest achievement, however.

As already recorded, III/JG 27 arrived in Sicily on 5 May, joining Müncheberg's unit in its activities, and claiming five victories by the 20th. All but one of these were credited to the unit's leading pilot, *Oblt.* Erbo Graf von Kageneck. At the end of May, most remaining Luftwaffe units in Sicily were withdrawn for redeployment to the invasion force on the Russian frontier, but 7/JG 26 was ordered to Africa to reinforce I/JG 27. Müncheberg, now holder of the *Ritterkreuz mit Eichenlaub*, had shot down 19 aircraft over Malta and Yugoslavia, increasing his personal score to 43. Although junior to Neumann, he was treated as an honoured guest by the latter.

Immediately after the arrival of 7/JG 26 at the start of June 1941, the British launched their unsuccessful Operation 'Battleaxe', and for a few days fighting in the air was fierce. The four *Staffeln* of Bf109Es were backed only by 8/ZG 26, the other two units of III *Gruppe* having moved to the north side of the Mediterranean at this stage, to provide an air defence of Greece and Crete. Despite their small numbers, the German fighters were to gain an immediate ascendency over the Hurricanes by which they were mainly faced, and the losses inflicted on the RAF during that period were severe.

The latter part of June and the month of July saw desultory action, mainly concentrated over Allied convoys attempting to supply the defenders of Tobruk, which was still in a state of siege. The first American-built Curtiss Tomahawk fighters had begun to appear over the front early in June, the Germans finding them to be dangerous opponents for the Bf109E. On 29 July, Müncheberg shot down two Tomahawks to raise his score in Africa to five, but 7/JG 26 then ended its overseas detachment, returning to Europe to join the parent *Geschwader* in western France.

The stalemate which existed on the Libyan–Egyptian frontier during the summer of 1941 was to be the longest of the whole African war; at that stage the forces of each antagonist were relatively small, and the struggle to build up a sufficient margin of strength for an all-out offensive was a slow business for both sides. Late in July III/ZG 26, mainly employed now in long-range escort and strafing duties, recorded its 33rd aerial victory since arriving in the Mediterranean area.

To meet the threat posed by the Tomahawks, the *Staffeln* of I/JG 27 began withdrawing to Germany one at a time during September, to re-equip with the latest Bf109F-4s, but at the same time reinforcements were arriving in the shape of II/JG 27, also newly equipped with the F variant. This unit had claimed 85 victories during 1940, 17 over Greece during April 1941, and than 39 in 10 days in Russia. *Gruppenkommandeur* was *Hptm.* Wolfgang Lippert (25 victories), and *Oblt.* Gustav Rödel, who had now raised his own score to 20, led 4 *Staffel*, the first to arrive in the area. The *Gruppe* then boasted at least 6 other pilots with scores in excess of 5, amongst whom the most successful were *Obfw.* Erwin Sawallisch with 19 and *Obfw.* Otto Schulz with 9. The unit went into action at the start of October with immediate success, Rödel particularly doing well.

Rommel was now preparing for a new offensive designed to capture Tobruk and thereby put an end to the drain on his resources caused by the need to split his forces between the besieged port and the frontier. In readiness for this move, III/ZG 26 reassembled at Derna as a complete unit, while a fighter-bomber *Staffel*, 10 (*Jabo*)/JG 27, also arrived from Europe, equipped with Bf109Es. However, before the new German offensive could be started the British struck. On 18 November 1941, Operation 'Crusader' began the biggest Allied offensive of the war so far. Rommel was taken by surprise, but countered quickly, and for some days the issue stood in the balance as opposing armour clashed. Overhead each side joined in the most intense air battles to date, and some hard combats were fought. On 20 November an unescorted formation of nine Martin Marylands was intercepted by aircraft of I/JG 27, only the small number of the attackers keeping the bombers' losses down to four, three of which fell to *Ltn.* Hans-Arnold Stahlschmidt.

On 22 November the opposing fighters clashed twice in the heaviest battle for air superiority yet fought in Africa. Numerically the Luftwaffe came off best, shooting down 10 Tomahawks and 4 Blenheims for the loss of 6 Bf109s, 2 from I *Gruppe* and 4 from II *Gruppe*. Even this relatively low rate of loss could not be borne for long by the small German force available, as the RAF now enjoyed substantial numerical superiority. Thereafter the Germans rarely met the more manoeuvrable British fighters in the traditional dog-fight. Instead they relied on the superior altitude performance of the Bf109F to allow them to fly above the RAF formations, diving on stragglers or unwary squadrons to pick them off at will. Another bad loss was

had taken an increasing toll of Axis shipping in the Mediterranean. Consequently, in order to support Rommel, *Fliegerkorps* II was ordered from the central Russian front to Sicily on 28 November 1941, to renew the *Blitz* on the intrepid defenders of the island. Fighter complement of this *Korps* included all three *Gruppen* of *Maj.* Günther von Maltzahn's JG 53 '*Pik As*', plus II/JG 3. Aircraft from these units began arriving in early December, and were ready for action by the middle of the month.

* * *

Günther von Maltzahn was at that time one of the Luftwaffe's leading fighter pilots; decorated with the *Ritterkreuz mit Eichenlaub*, he had been in action since the start of the war, and had a score already approaching 50. In his *Stabschwarm* was a

suffered on 23 November however, when *Hptm.* Lippert, *Kommandeur* of II/JG 27, was shot down and captured, only to die of his injuries a few days later in a British hospital. III/ZG 26 was also having a hard time of it, being badly mauled by Hurricanes and Tomahawks on several occasions, and losing its *Kommandeur*, *Maj.* Karl Kaschka, in combat on 5 December.

Meanwhile, renewed activity had once again shown the difficulty of supplying the Axis forces in Africa, while Malta remained a base for Allied offensive operations. After its battering early in 1941, the island had steadily recovered, and acting as a home for submarines, bombers, and destroyers,

Operating over Malta from December 1941 onwards was JG 53. II *Gruppe* of this *Geschwader* flew from Sicily for almost a full year thereafter. Here aircraft of the *Geschwader* are seen on Comiso airfield during 1942, that in the foreground being flown by *Ltn.* Hermann Harnisch, a fourteen victory *Experte*. (H. Harnisch)

promising young *Leutnant*, Franz Schiess, who had gained 15 victories over Russia. I *Gruppe* had just been taken over by an ex-*Zerstörerflieger* and *Ritterkreuzträger*, *Hptm.* Herbert Kaminski, who had about five victories to his credit. The adjutant of this *Gruppe* was *Ltn.* Klaus Quaet-Faslem, who was also one of its leading pilots, as were *Oblt.* Friedrich-Karl 'Tutti' Müller, *Staffelkapitän* of 1 *Staffel*, whose score stood at 20, and *Ltn.* Wolfgang

During the various *Afrika Korps* retreats across Libya, many unserviceable aircraft had to be abandoned. Here a Bf109G *Schwarze* 6 is seen on Gambut airfield late in 1942. It was subsequently given the RAF serial MK849. (via F. F. Smith)

Tonne, who had been doing well in Russia following five victories during the 1940 campaigns. In II *Gruppe* were several experienced pilots who had been building up their scores, notably *Ltn.* Gerhard Michalski, Fritz Dinger and *Feldwebel* Herbert Rollwage, although no pilots in this *Gruppe* yet wore the coveted *Ritterkreuz*.

Undoubtedly the leading element of JG 53 at that time was III *Gruppe*, led by *Hptm.* Wolfe-Dietrich Wilcke, *Ritterkreuzträger* with 33 victories, the unit including many leading pilots. Among the notables

were *Oblt.* Altendorf (15 victories), *Staffelkapitän* of 7 *Staffel, Oblt.* Franz Götz (30 victories) leading 8 *Staffel, Ltn.* Herbert Schramm and *Ltn.* Hermann Neuhoff with 37 each, *Obfw.* Werner Stumpf with 24, and at least 5 more with good scores. II/JG 3, the fourth *Jagdgruppe* in the *Korps*, had just been taken over by *Hptm.* Karl-Heinz Krahl, an ex-*Legion Condor* pilot who had been awarded the *Ritterkreuz* in November 1940 after his 15th victory. Just posted in from JG 2 in the west, his score was now around 20. Krahl's leading pilot was *Fw.* Walter

A shattered Bf109F of II/JG 27 following a crash-landing in the desert. The aircraft has been stripped by souvenir hunters—note that both the swastika on the fin and victory bars marked on the rudder fabric have been cut away. (via F. F. Smith)

Arriving in Africa just before the Alamein battle of October 1942 to reinforce the *Jabogruppe Afrika* in the ground attack rôle, III/ZG 1 saw only limited action before re-formation and re-equipment with Me210s. Here one of its Bf109Es, W.Nr 6431, is seen here after crash-landing during the battle. (IWM)

Throughout the 1941–42 period the Bf110s of III/ZG 26 made a useful contribution both as escorts to transport aircraft carrying supplies across the Mediterranean from Crete and Greece to Africa, and in the ground attack rôle. Here a trio of the unit's aircraft is prepared for flight on a Cretan airfield in 1942. In the background is 3U-DD.

Ohlrogge, one of the oldest Luftwaffe pilots still on operations, who had just received the *Ritterkreuz* after his 39th victory. Several other pilots had much experience, while a number of newer members of the *Gruppe* were proving most promising, including young *Ltn.* Joachim Kirschner, who would soon gain his first victories over Malta. Also on the strength of JG 53 at that time—*Gruppe* uncertain—was *Oblt.* Kurt Brändle, who had claimed 14 victories during 1940, and whose score had now risen to around 40.

As soon as these new units had arrived however, III/JG 53 was despatched to Libya to aid the units of JG 27 in the fighting there, which was now going badly for the ground forces. The unit fought its first combat in Africa on 11 December, and was soon claiming regularly.

In an effort to fly in urgently needed fuel, Junkers Ju52/3m transports made the long flight from Crete to Libya, heavily laden with barrels. Lacking sufficient long-range fighters, the RAF utilized

III/JG 53 alternated between Sicily and North Africa throughout 1942, playing an important part in the fighting over Malta and the desert. Here two of the unit's Bf109Gs are seen in flight over the sea during late 1942. The nearest, apparently *Rote* 1, is believed to be flown by the *Experte Oblt.* Franz Götz, who had sixty victories at this time. This particular aircraft featured a red rudder with sixty white victory bars marked thereon.

Maryland bombers in this role to intercept them, but during mid-December III/ZG 26 joined Ju88 night fighters in making a number of sorties to counter this action. Several of the British aircraft were thereby intercepted and shot down.

Meanwhile the *Afrika Korps* was steadily retreating across Libya, and air units were forced to move back, bases in the Tmimi area being evacuated for others at Martuba and Derna. At this stage a fourth full *Gruppe* of Bf109Fs arrived in Africa, this being III/JG 27, bringing the whole *Geschwader* together for the first time in many months. The unit had been very successful in the past, with 134 victories during 1940, 5 over Malta in May 1941, and then 220 in Russia. Several successful pilots were with III *Gruppe* but the most outstanding was *Oblt.* Erbo Graf von Kageneck—at that time *Geschwader* top scorer with 65 victories, and recipient of the *Ritterkreuz mit Eichenlaub.* As well as III *Gruppe,* the *Geschwaderstab* with the *Kommodore, Maj.* Bernhard Woldenga, arrived in Africa.

Despite this increased strength, a number of blows hit the German fighters once more. On 13 December *Obfw.* Albert Espenlaub, one of I/JG 27's most successful pilots in Africa, was shot down and captured: he had claimed fourteen victories since April. Two days later III/JG 53 lost *Oblt.* Altendorf,

also as a prisoner, while on Christmas Eve the great von Kageneck was mortally wounded in combat with British fighters. *Hauptmann* Thomas Steinberger, the new *Kommandeur* of III/ZG 26, was also lost on 24 December.

On 17 December, following the entry into action of III/JG 27, III/JG 53 returned to Sicily, where it was followed a few days later by two of the *Staffeln* of ZG 26. By this time the *Zerstörergruppe* had suffered heavily; since arriving in the Mediterranean, 11 aircrew had been killed in action, 27 were missing, 9 were prisoners, 16 had been wounded, and 6 killed in accidents. This was a rate of personnel attrition approaching 100 per cent in a year!

Meanwhile the new *Blitz* on Malta from bases in Sicily was well under way by late December, claims for upwards of twenty British aircraft having been submitted by the turn of the year. The *Jagdflieger* continued to hit the outclassed Hurricanes hard during the opening month of 1942, and before long these aircraft were hardly able to offer an effective defence, despite the arrival of further reinforcements. The numbers of Axis aircraft failing to return from attacks on the island fell considerably.

RISING STARS

Pushed right back to El Agheila by early January 1942, Rommel received badly needed fuel and supplies as the assault on Malta began to take effect, and in mid-month he was able to launch a counter-attack, driving the British halfway across Cyrenaica to a line running south from Gazala. By this time, some of the JG 27 pilots were beginning to achieve some very impressive results with the Bf109F, having become expert at their trade. On 14 January 1942 *Hptm.* Erich Gerlitz and *Uffz.* Horst Reuter of II/JG 27 bounced Hurricanes of No. 94 Squadron, RAF, over Bir el Ginn. Gerlitz shot down one (his 11th desert victory, and 14th of the war) but then had to withdraw with engine trouble. Reuter meanwhile attacked the rest of the formation and claimed four shot down. Owing to lack of witnesses he had difficulty in getting these confirmed, but in fact he had actually brought down no less than six Hurricanes! These claims raised Reuter's total in Africa to 15; with a confirmed score of 21, all but

one of them over the desert, he was shot down in May 1942 and became a prisoner.

The leading lights of JG 27 at that time were Gerhard Homuth and Hans-Joachim Marseille of I *Gruppe* and Otto Schulz of II *Gruppe*. Since November, Marseille had claimed 11 victories, and on 8 February he added 4 more to become desert top scorer with 40 in Africa, thereby overtaking Homuth, who had 39. Schulz was close behind with 37. Next day Homuth got his 40th, but on the 12th, Marseille claimed 4 fighters in 8 minutes. Then on the 15th came Schulz's big day. Taking off during a strafing attack on Martuba, he shot down 5 Kittyhawks, including that flown by one of the leading RAF desert aces, Sqn. Ldr. E. M. 'Imshi' Mason: the unlucky British unit was again No. 94 Squadron which had just exchanged its Hurricanes for the American fighters. Marseille and Schulz were then each awarded the *Ritterkreuz*, the latter returning to Germany to undertake officer training. He would return late in May as an *Oberleutnant*. These were not by any means the first such awards to be made to the *Geschwader* during the period: in June 1941 Homuth and Rödel had each been decorated, while in July Franzisket and Redlich of I *Gruppe* also joined the ranks of the *Ritterkreuzträger*.

As the battle continued to rage over Malta, the Luftwaffe retained its early ascendency. During March the island's outdated Hurricanes were reinforced by the first Spitfires to serve in the fighter role outside the UK, these having been flown in to the island from the deck of HMS *Eagle*. Although fighting then became tougher, most advantages remained with the Germans—a steady toll of the defenders continued to be taken and at the same time the island's offensive capacity was progressively crippled. However on 10 April III/JG 53 lost *Ltn.* Hermann Neuhoff (40 victories), who was shot down by his own wingman by accident to become a prisoner only a day or two before the award of his *Ritterkreuz* was announced. Four days later, *Hptm.* Krahl, *Kommandeur* of II/JG 3, was shot down by ground fire while strafing Luqa airfield, and was killed. Kurt Brändle was posted in from JG 53 as his replacement.

In Africa JG 27 faced a new hazard on 21 March, when Colonel David Stirling's famous Special Air

Service commandos raided the airfield at Martuba. The defenders were successful in foiling the attack on this occasion, subsequently strafing the intruders as they fled from the area; but the attack was yet another factor in the strain of operating under the conditions prevailing in Libya.

The spring months of 1942 remained fairly quiet, and during April a special *Schwarm* of four Bf109s was despatched to Crete by III/JG 27. These machines shot down several reconnaissance and bombing aircraft there during the rest of the year. In mid-April 6/JG 3 paid a brief visit to the desert, and flew a few sorties before returning to Sicily without having added to its score tally. The month also saw the first anniversary of I/JG 27's arrival in Africa, and suitable festivities were arranged to mark the occasion.

By early May both sides were almost ready to resume the offensive, *Fliegerführer Afrika* having to hand 92 Bf109Fs of I, II and III/JG 27; eight Bf109Es of the *Jabostaffel*; 12 Bf110s of 7/ZG 26; 11 Ju88Cs of 12/LG 1 (a recently formed *Zerstörerstaffel* which had been raised from the bomber *Lehrgeschwader* 1), and 9 night fighter Ju88Cs of 2/NJG 2. On 20 May

Bf109Gs of II/JG 53 in Sicily at the time of the Tunisian invasion by Anglo-American forces, late 1942/early 1943. In the background is a Bf110D of III/ZG 26, and a number of Junkers Ju52/3m transports.

III/JG 53 returned to Libya, *Maj.* Gerlitz from JG 27 being posted in to command this *Gruppe* when *Hptm.* Wilcke was posted to the *Geschwaderstab* of JG 3 in Russia. Gerlitz's II/JG 27 was taken over by Gustav Rödel. A few days later the other two *Staffeln* of III/ZG 26 arrived, joining with 12/LG 1 and a *Stukageschwader* to form *Gefechtsverbände Sigel* for special ground support duties. III/ZG 26 also undertook some night interceptions over Africa and gained a few victories. The most successful pilot in these operations was *Oblt.* Alfred Wehmeyer, who claimed 3 bombers at night by late May to raise his total in Africa to 5 at least, and his score for the war to 18. On 1 June, the day after his final nocturnal success against a Wellington, Wehmeyer was killed when his aircraft suffered a direct hit from a Bofors shell during a low-level attack west of Tobruk. He was later awarded the *Ritterkreuz* posthumously.

The despatch of III/JG 53 from Sicily marked a general run-down of strength there, II/JG 3 and I/JG 53 returning to Russia to take part in the summer offensive. This left only II/JG 53 on the island, together with the *Stabschwarm*, and a handful of night fighters and Italian fighter units which moved in to keep up the pressure as the Luftwaffe withdrew. During June the arrival of a major convoy and a renewal of offensive operations from

Personnel of II/JG 53 prepare equipment at their base in Sicily, ready for a move to Tunisia. In the background is one of the unit's Bf109Gs, and a Ju52/3m.

Malta resulted in the despatch of I/JG 77 to Sicily from south Russia on 6 July. This unit had just been taken over by *Hptm*. Heinz 'Pritzl' Bär, one of the real 'characters' of the *Jagdflieger*. Handsome, rakish, charming and witty, Bär was extremely popular with all who knew him. He was also an outstanding fighter pilot who had been in action since 1939 and who had been the top-scoring NCO pilot of 1940. His total now stood at around 120, and with the *Schwerten* (Swords) to his *Ritterkreuz mit Eichenlaub*, he was the highest scoring and most highly decorated fighter pilot yet to serve in the Mediterranean zone. His *Staffelkapitän* included *Hptm*. Fritz Geisshardt who, it will be recalled, had flown over Greece and Crete in 1941 with the same unit—then designated I(J)/LG 2. Geisshardt now had 82 victories, and he had just added the *Eichenlaub* to his *Ritterkreuz*. Besides Geisshardt there was also *Oblt*. Siegfried Freytag, *Ritterkreuzträger* with some 49 victories.

I/JG 77's arrival in Sicily coincided with the delivery of further Spitfires to Malta, resulting in some fairly sustained fighting over the island during mid-July. The reduced German presence meant that the *Jagdflieger* were now frequently joined on their missions by MC202 and Re2001 fighters of the *Regia Aeronautica*.

* * *

In the desert, Rommel had struck first, attacking the British main defences at Gazala with his infantry, whilst armour attempted an outflanking move to the south. The whole desert erupted in the heaviest and most prolonged battle yet seen. In the air, RAF fighter-bombers were thrown in in force, in a desperate effort to slow down the Panzers and save the situation. Flying high above on *Freie Jagd* sorties, the German *Jagdflieger* enjoyed almost endless opportunities to increase their scores, the unfortunate Kittybombers and Hurribombers falling in droves. The battle raged to and fro as Free

French forces at Bir Hacheim fought a dogged defence of the southern flank, but as May wore on into June the advantage passed inexorably to the *Afrika Korps*. At the height of the battle, Edu Neumann of I/JG 27 was promoted to become *Geschwaderkommodore*, his place at the head of I *Gruppe* being taken by Gerhard Homuth; Marseille now took command of 3 *Staffel*.

As the British forces began withdrawing eastwards, Luftwaffe units moved after them, I/JG 27 and III/JG 53 going to Derna on 14 June. To compound the problems faced by the RAF, a large convoy now attempted to sail from Alexandria to Malta, requiring support from the hard-pressed Western Desert Air Force as Axis units from both Africa and Crete took up the attack. At this very moment III/JG 53 was ordered to fly to Athens/Eleusis airfield in Greece. En route five aircraft of 8 *Staffel* intercepted Beaufort torpedo-bombers which were on their way to attack Italian Fleet units threatening the convoy. The Messerschmitts fell on the bombers at once, and seven or eight were claimed shot down. Later in the day the movement order was changed and the whole

Gruppe, minus the *Jabostaffel* (which had now also reached Africa), was directed to move to Sicily instead. On the 18th this order was rescinded also, and the *Gruppe* was fragmented between Greece, Crete and Sicily until it finally arrived back in Libya to resume operations on the 20th.

The *Gruppen* of JG 27 continued to move forward, and by the 22nd, I and III *Gruppen*, plus III/JG 53, were at Gambut. They moved on to Fuka before the end of the month, as the British were pushed back into Egypt, Tobruk falling to the Axis on 21 June. During the last burst of fighting before the port fell, Marseille had excelled himself. On 17 June he shot down four Kittyhawks to raise his score to 99. Then, encouraged by cries of '*Und nur den Hundertsten, Jochen!*' from his comrades, he brought down a lone Hurricane to become the first German to be credited with shooting down 100 British aircraft. A further victory followed during the flight back to base, and on landing, Marseille was at once ordered to Berlin to receive the award of the *Schwerten* directly from the *Führer*'s hands. The award of the *Eichenlaub* to him had been announced only twelve days earlier. On the very same day, the other great *Experte*, Otto Schulz, shot down his fifty-first victim—a Hurricane—but was then himself shot down by a Kittyhawk and killed. The Kittyhawk was flown by

Pilots of II/JG 53 rush to their Bf109Gs for an *Alarmstart* in the early 1943 period.

one of the RAF's rising aces, Canadian F/Sgt. J. F. Edwards of No. 260 Squadron.

Throughout July the fighting continued at full pace as the Axis troops struggled to break the line which the British were now holding across the narrow neck of desert between El Alamein and the salt marshes of the Qattara Depression. The first USAAF aircraft began to appear over the front in support of the RAF, including B-24 Liberator bombers, which operated by day. The first of these formidable aircraft to be shot down was claimed by *Fw.* Günther Steinhausen of I/JG 27 on 9 July. The period 26 May–26 July had seen some of the fastest scoring of the whole desert war for JG 27, but it had also had 66 Bf109s destroyed by enemy action— almost 100 per cent of the *Geschwader*'s normal operational strength.

Following the heavy fighting over Malta in mid-July, the latter part of the month and early August had been fairly quiet. The approach of a major convoy from the west (Operation 'Pedestal') on 12 August, carrying supplies and fuel for the island's garrison, was the sign for renewed activity for a couple of days. Thereafter, so little action was instituted that Spitfires from Malta started to appear over the Sicilian coast, undertaking offensive sweeps and fighter-bomber nuisance raids.

Generally August was a relatively quiet month in

Africa too, as both sides attempted to reinforce as quickly as possible. The two *Jabostaffeln* of III/JG 27 and III/JG 53 were active however, flying together as the *Jabogruppe Afrika*. They were joined late in the month by III/ZG 1, a newly formed ground attack unit which arrived in Africa with a mixture of Bf109Es and Bf110s, and by the end of the month the Luftwaffe fighter force in Africa was at its strongest ever. The whole of JG 27 with 73 Bf109Fs and 12 Bf109E *Jabo* was available, together with two dozen aircraft of III/JG 53 and seven Dornier Do17Zs employed for *Zerstörer* operations by a recently formed unit, 10/ZG 26. In Crete were the three Bf109Fs of JG 27's *Jagdkommando*, together with the 46 Bf110s of III/ZG 26.

An unusual success occurred on 7 August when *Uffz.* Bernd Schneider of II/JG 27, flying an interdiction mission behind the British lines, shot down a Bristol Bombay transport carrying General Gott to take up his new post as commander of the 8th Army. Gott was killed, his place subsequently being filled by a relatively unknown officer, Bernard Montgomery. On two occasions during mid-August the RAF launched heavy attacks on the Axis fighter airfields in the Fuka area, but while these resulted in heavy combats overhead, the damage on the ground was not nearly as severe as the British might have hoped. British and American heavy bombers also launched a number of attacks on Crete, several fierce battles with defending Bf109s and 110s developing, and several victories were claimed by III/ZG 26.

A Bf109G of an unknown unit (possibly JG 77) is prepared for take-off. Note splinter camouflage, white wingtips, and lack of white rear fuselage band.

Bf110D of III/ZG 26 in flight.

FACING DEFEAT

On 31 August the *Afrika Korps* launched a new offensive against the southern end of the British line at Alem el Halfa. The 8th Army was expecting this move however, and was ready for Rommel's troops, who were brought to a swift halt and forced to retreat. The Western Desert Air Force was thrown in in strength and while the *Jagdflieger* were thereby given another tremendous opportunity to gain dazzling personal successes in numbers of British fighters shot down, they were quite unable to defend the ground troops from bombing attacks, which harried the Panzers and shattered the soft-skinned vehicles bringing up supplies and ammunition. Marseille had returned from leave in time for this battle, and on 1 September enjoyed his greatest day, claiming no less than seventeen victories during the course of three missions.

Despite the increased Luftwaffe fighter strength, the Allies had built up their forces to a much greater extent, and Spitfires were now appearing in growing numbers. Owing to the renewed depredations of Malta-based aircraft and submarines, German supplies of all types were critically short, none more so than petrol for tanks and aircraft. Even as Marseille gained his great success on 1 September, *Maj.* Roland Bohrt, *Kommandeur* of the newly arrived III/ZG 1, was shot down in his Bf109E and mortally wounded.

Constantly outnumbered, worn out by continual operations, and regularly bombed on their own airfields, the German pilots were beginning to suffer a deterioration in their morale. On 3 September Hans-Arnold Stahlschmidt, one of I/JG 27's leading pilots with fifty-nine victories, wrote home:

'I don't know what fate awaits me. Perhaps things are going other than our thoughts and wishes desire. But, if *it* should happen, then I know I have done my duty with all my heart.'

Stahlschmidt may well have had a premonition of his fate, for four days later he was shot down and killed in a combat with Spitfires of No. 601 Squadron. Karl von Lieres, another of the unit's *Experten*, was forced to carry out a crash-landing at the same time, and only the day before, Günther Steinhausen had been brought down to his death by Hurricanes of No. 127 Squadron after forty victories. It was clearly too much, and on 8 September I *Gruppe* was rested.

The unit was soon back in action however, and on 15 September Marseille claimed 7 Kittyhawks to raise his score to 158—the highest total ever to be claimed against the Western Allies throughout the war. The next day he was promoted to become the youngest *Hauptmann* in the Luftwaffe, but more tragedy was at hand for I/JG 27. On 30 September, flying a new Bf109G, Marseille's aircraft suffered a lubrication fire. He baled out of the inverted fighter with the cockpit shrouded in thick smoke, his body striking the tailplane, and he fell unconscious to his death. After this blow, I *Gruppe*'s morale sank to rock bottom. To provide a change of scene the unit was ordered to Sicily on a short detachment at the start of October. At the same time the *Jabogruppe* and III/ZG 1 were withdrawn to form a new unit, *Schlachtgeschwader* 2 (consisting of two *Gruppen*), and a new III/ZG 1, to equip with the latest Messerschmitt Me210 *Zerstörer*.

On 9 October another big Allied air attack was launched on the fighter bases at Fuka, and this time thirteen of III/JG 53's Bf109Fs were badly damaged on the ground. A few days later this unit lost *Obfw.* Werner Stumpf, one of its top pilots who had recently been awarded the *Ritterkreuz*. Stumpf had forty-seven victories to his credit when he fell victim to anti-aircraft fire.

Meanwhile, early in October, I/JG 53 had returned to Sicily from Russia; and a few days later on the 11th, another great assault was launched against the island of Malta in an effort to subdue the defences and reduce the offensive capability based there, thus allowing more supplies to reach Rommel. This attack was the largest yet mounted, but the reinforced defenders now had adequate Spitfires to intercept every raid, and far from enjoying the measure of success achieved on previous occasions, so great was the rate of attrition suffered by the German bombers that after a few days they had to be withdrawn from further daylight operations. Heavy fighting between the opposing fighters continued for several more days, both sides suffering substantial losses. Units involved were I and II/JG 53, I/JG 77 and I/JG 27. When the assault ended, two pilots who had done particularly well during the whole summer and autumn period were Gerhard Michalski of II/JG 53 with 26 victories, and Siegfried Freytag of I/JG 77 with somewhere between 20 and 30; it remains a matter of conjecture at present which of these pilots had become Luftwaffe top scorer over Malta. Fritz Geisshardt of I/JG 77 had also done well, claiming 9 Spitfires during the same period.

Just as the attack on Malta was repulsed, Montgomery launched his great offensive at El Alamein on 24 October. The battle quickly developed into a week-long slogging match during which the Axis reserves were drawn in and destroyed. Initially only *Stab*, II and III/JG 27, III/JG 53, the new I/Sch.G 2, and a handful of *Zerstörer* were available, although I/JG 27 returned on the 27th. It was now intended to replace the *Geschwader* in Africa with JG 77, and the unit was accompanied from Sicily by I/JG 77. With the arrival of these two *Gruppen*, III/JG 53 returned to the parent unit in Sicily.

Next day III/JG 77 arrived direct from Russia under the command of *Hptm.* Kurt Ubben (95 victories). This unit too had experienced *Staffelkapitän* serving with it—*Hptm.* Wolf-Dietrich Huy (40 victories), *Oblt.* Emil Omert (55 victories) and *Oblt.* Helmut Goedert (25 victories). Ubben, Huy and Omert had all taken part in the Greek and Cretan campaigns the previous year. The *Geschwaderstab* soon followed, led by none other than Joachim Müncheberg, now the *Kommodore* with the rank of *Major* and a score of over 100. The *Geschwader* had enjoyed great success in Russia, and the pilots' 'tails were high': they intended to show the poor fellows in JG 27 'how it should be done'. They were soon left in little doubt of the new conditions they now faced, however, for on the 29th, the day after his arrival, Huy was shot down by Spitfires and became a prisoner. On the same day I/JG 27's long-serving *Hptm.* Ludwig Franzisket (37 victories) was also shot down. He baled out and broke his leg.

At the start of November, I/JG 53—which had just been taken over by *Hptm.* 'Tutti' Müller, whose score had risen to over 100 in Russia—flew to Tobruk on a brief and uneventful detachment. A few days later Axis resistance at El Alamein crumbled, and Rommel began a fighting withdrawal out of Egypt and across Cyrenaica. On the 3rd, the fighter units left Fuka for Sidi Barrani, Menastir and Gambut. II/JG 27, reduced to only three serviceable aircraft which were handed to JG 77, withdrew to Gambut to receive new Bf109G-6s, which were now arriving from Germany. On the 6th, the *Gruppe* was operational again, but two days later came news of the Anglo-American landings in French north-west Africa, far in the rear. The die was now cast and the Luftwaffe's days in Africa were numbered. On the 12th, *Stab* plus I and III/JG 27 were ordered to leave Africa, the two former units to Germany, the latter to Crete and Greece. All Bf109s were handed over to units of JG 77 which, with II/JG 27, now withdrew to Magrun.

The retreat continued, and by late November *Stab* plus I and III/JG 77 were at Arco Philaenorum with 39 Bf109s, while II/JG 27 was at Nofilia with 35. About half of these fighters were serviceable. At this time the re-formed III/ZG 1 was being re-equipped with Me210s while 10/ZG 26 was exchanging its remaining Do17Zs for Ju88Cs. Early in December II/JG 77 started to arrive. This was the *Geschwader*'s most successful *Gruppe*, with 1,300 victories—claimed mainly in Russia. It was led by *Hptm.* Anton Mader (over 50 victories), and had amongst its *Staffelkapitän Hptm.* Anton Hackl with 118 victories and *Oblt.* Lutz-Wilhelm Burkhardt with 53. With the arrival of this final *Gruppe* of JG 77, II/JG 27 now ceased operations and left for Italy—much to the delight of its personnel. By this time JG 27 had claimed 1,166 victories in Africa, 588 of them by I *Gruppe*. Additionally III/JG 53 had claimed a further 113.

With the desert to themselves, the pilots of JG 77 now began to get into the swing of operations with some success, and on 19 December, I *Gruppe* was able to celebrate its 1,000th victory of the war. As the year drew to a close, however, II *Gruppe* took a knock: in two of its first African combats on 30 December the unit lost several aircraft and three pilots to RAF Kittyhawks. I/Sch.G 1 which was being escorted also lost at least one Bf109.

As previously mentioned, on 8 November 1942 British and American troops landed in French Morocco, and at two locations in Algeria—Algiers and Oran. From Algiers British troops pushed eastwards, soon crossing the Tunisian frontier and approaching the twin ports of Tunis and Bizerta. Acting with great speed, *Feldmarschal* Albert Kesselring, Luftwaffe commander and senior officer in the Mediterranean, sent in troops in Ju52/3ms,

backed by Ju87s and by Bf109s of I/JG 53, all units flying from Sicily to Tunis airport. On 12 November III/JG 53 followed, and was in combat with RAF Spitfires over the Tunisian mountains by the 14th. Part of III/ZG 2 also arrived for ground attack duties. This recently formed unit had just arrived from Germany equipped with Bf109Es and a few Fw190s. In February 1943 it would be redesignated III/SKG 10. III/ZG 26 flew to Sicily from Crete to escort further shuttle flights of transport aircraft to Tunisia, joining III/ZG 1 which was preparing for similar duties.

British and American fighter units with Spitfires and P-40s, soon followed by P-38s, were arriving in Algeria in considerable numbers; and while the Luftwaffe enjoyed better airfields closer to the front, shorter supply lines, and improved early warning systems, it was clear that more fighters would be needed. Consequently, on 14 November II/JG 51 arrived at Bizerta from Russia, led by *Hptm.* Hartmann Grasser (92 victories), and including several other highly successful pilots on its strength. It was soon followed by II/JG 2 from France. This unit was equipped with Focke-Wulf Fw190As and was the first fighter unit to operate these aircraft in the Mediterranean area. 11/JG 2 also arrived to reinforce II/JG 53 in Sicily, the *Staffel*, led by *Oblt.* Julius Meimberg, being absorbed into this unit together with its Bf109s. II/JG 51 was similarly reinforced by the arrival of 11/JG 26.

A 'gaggle' of Bf109Gs of JG 53 in *Staffel* strength pass low over their airfield, *c.* early 1943.

Luftwaffe pilots on a Mediterranean airfield await the call to action, close to their Bf109Gs. These aircraft have spinner rings in *Staffel* colours.

The campaign which now began in Tunisia was to see almost constant aerial activity for the next six months, and was to give the Luftwaffe virtually the last taste of holding the whip hand over Anglo-American fighters. The units in the Tunis area were now faced for the first time with regular escorted raids by American heavy bombers, B-17s with P-38 and P-40 escorts flying from Algeria to attack the Tunisian ports and airfields, and other targets. The big bombers proved to be difficult opponents and many of the tactics later widely used over Europe were formulated here. One of the first B-17s to be shot down fell to *Oberstleutnant* von Maltzahn, *Kommodore* of JG 53, after a long combat on 28 November. As American troops crossed the frontier further south, a single *Staffel* from III/JG 53 was sent down to Gabes, but generally the battle line in Tunisia had hardened by the beginning of December, and harsh winter weather brought most movement on the ground to a halt.

During those early weeks some considerable successes were gained by the *Jagdflieger*: the inexperienced Americans in their P-38s and P-40s were cut to pieces on several occasions, while British Spitfire squadrons were savagely mauled during a number of raids on the Bone area. On 4 December, aircraft of II/JG 53—which had just taken over from III/JG 53 in Tunisia—joined by elements of II/JG 2, caught an unescorted formation of 11 Bristol Bisley bombers over northern Tunisia, and shot every one down, the newly arrived *Oblt.* Meimberg being credited with three.

In January 1943 Rommel's forces were forced to evacuate Tripoli, and began crossing the border into southern Tunisia, taking up positions behind the old French defences at Mareth. With JG 77 in the south and II/JG 2 and II/JG 51 having moved to central Tunisia, air battles were now waged over the entire country. Some fierce Luftwaffe attacks over Bone at the turn of the year resulted in some very hard fighting, and for the *Jagdflieger* this period brought the first losses of some of the leading *Experten* in Tunisia. The first to fall was the current top scorer, *Fw.* Anton Hafner of II/JG 51, who was shot down by RAF Spitfires on 2 January 1943 after claiming his 20th victory in Africa, a P-38. Hafner was removed to hospital with serious wounds which would keep him out of action for some six months.

On 12 January, an American bombing attack on Gabes in the southern part of central Tunisia brought up the newly arrived Bf109s of JG 77 to give battle. *Ltn.* Johannes Badum (54 victories) of

II/JG 77 fell victim to the P-38 escort. Slightly to the north on this same date, *Oblt.* Hans Heydrich, a *Staffelkapitän* in II/JG 51, was shot down by US P-40s. The next day JG 77 was to enjoy great success during a raid on one of its own airfields at Bir Dufan by Desert Air Force Baltimores. Three bombers and 10 escorting Kittyhawks were claimed shot down, Anton Hackl of II *Gruppe* claiming 4 of the fighters, while Müncheberg, Bär and Freytag were all amongst the successful pilots. On the following day, the 14th, a further 3 bombers and 14 fighters were claimed in similar circumstances, this time Bär claiming 3 fighters and 'Kuddel' Ubben of III *Gruppe* 2, his 100th and 101st victories. In the Tunis area on the 13th however, *Ltn.* Wilhelm Crinius became another victim of Spitfires—this time American ones. The leading *Experte* of I/JG 53 had gained 114 victories, 14 of them in the Mediterranean area, receiving the *Ritterkreuz mit Eichenlaub*. He became a prisoner of war.

As it was likely to be some time before Montgomery had built up his forces to a point where they could assault the Mareth Line, Rommel sought ways to secure his rear supply lines. American and French forces were threatening to cut the north-south supply route in the Sfax region of central Tunisia, and despite pressure from the Axis forces in the north, this danger remained. Consequently, he launched his last African offensive, joined by elements from the north. His plan was little short of grandiose, calling for an advance through the Kasserine Pass into southern Algeria, followed by a northwards swing to destroy the Allied supply bases and rear areas around Constantine. In the event, the attack by his hardened desert veterans during February caught the inexperienced Americans off balance, and came close to succeeding. Lack of co-operation from Jürgen von Arnim, commander in the north, slowed him down, and in the end a hastily assembled and international force of Allied reinforcements was able to hold his drive on the western side of the pass.

During most of the battle poor weather prevented much aerial activity, but as it drew to a close, the clouds cleared a little and the aircraft poured back into the skies. JG 77 continued to enjoy some startling successes, despite being grotesquely

continued on page 33

Oberleutnant **Hans-Joachim Marseille, June 1942,** painted from a photograph. He wears tropical version of Luftwaffe sidecap, without commissioned rank piping; a privately acquired four-pocket black leather flying jacket; and Army-issue tropical trousers, with standard flying boots. The jacket bears his German Cross on the right breast, his Iron Cross 1st Class on the left, and rank epaulettes. Scarf colour speculative.

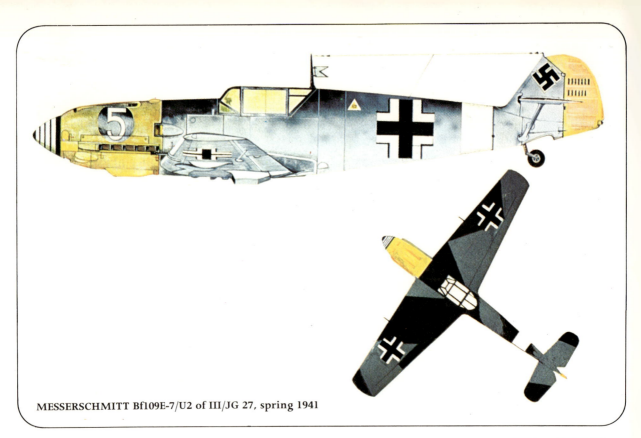

MESSERSCHMITT Bf109E-7/U2 of III/JG 27, spring 1941

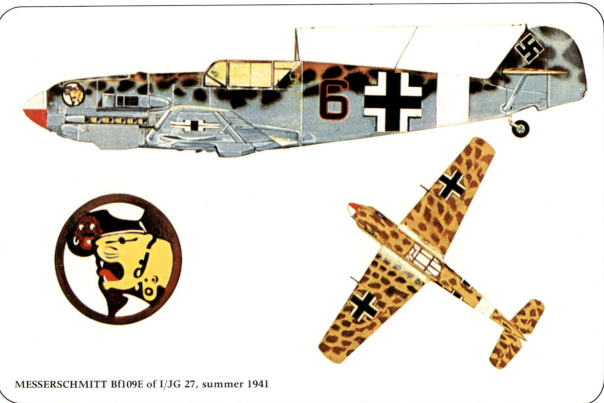

MESSERSCHMITT Bf109E of I/JG 27, summer 1941

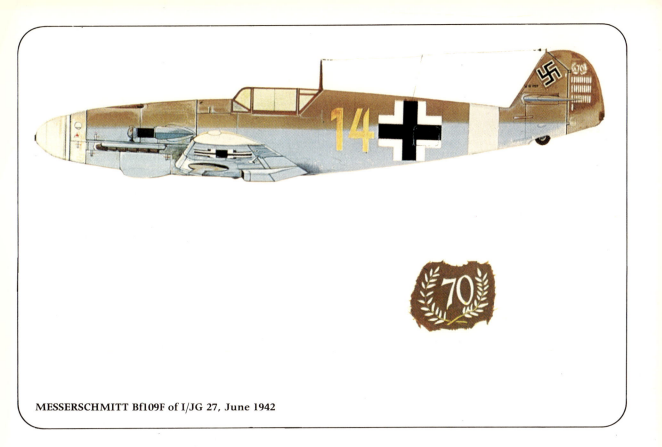

MESSERSCHMITT Bf109F of I/JG 27, June 1942

OPPOSITE TOP: Messerschmitt Bf109E-7/U2 of III/JG 27 flown by Erbo Graf von Kageneck, Balkans, spring 1941. Early Luftwaffe arrivals in the Mediterranean area bore standard European camouflage for a short period—in this case a splinter pattern of greys 74 and 75 on the upper surfaces and 76 white-blue on the undersides. The white rear fuselage band later became a standard identification marking for fighters, along with white wing tips, spinner and forward section of the engine cowling. The positioning of the individual aircraft number on the cowling on a circular background was common practice in III/JG 27 during this period. The radio mast pennant is presumed to be that of a flight commander, von Kageneck himself holding the rank of *Oberleutnant* at that time, with thirteen victories. He eventually went on to score sixty-seven before being killed in 1942.

OPPOSITE BOTTOM: Messerschmitt Bf109E of I/JG 27, North Africa, summer 1941. Within a few weeks of arrival in desert climes, those fighter units destined to remain for any length of time resprayed their machines in colours far better suited to their new operational area. This machine, of I/JG 27, has sand yellow 79 top surfaces and blue 78 below, the former being oversprayed with shade 80. There were, apparently, two shades of this colour, with either a brown or green cast and the former is shown here. The 'lion over Africa' badge of JG 27 was widely applied to the Bf109E, but in finish, individual fighters showed detail differences; it will be noted that the 'splatter' effect shown here on some blotches of 80 were in evidence on the original aircraft. The white spinner with two red segments indicated the second *Staffel* of I *Gruppe*, as did the colour of the number.

ABOVE: Messerschmitt Bf109F of I/JG 27 flown by *Oblt.* Hans Joachim Marseille, June 1942. One of a number of Bf109s flown by the top-scoring Luftwaffe fighter pilot in the desert, the drawing depicts the machine used to score victories 82 and 83 on 11 June 1942. The machine bears the widely used colour scheme of sand 79 and blue 78 with horizontal fuselage division and full white identification markings.

27

MESSERSCHMITT Bf109F of III/JG 53 *'Pik As'*, early 1942

PAGES 28–29: Messerschmitt Bf109F of III/JG 53 'Pik As' showing the scheme introduced early in 1942—overall sand 79 upper surfaces with blue 78 below. The vertical bar marking to denote III *Gruppe* appears aft of the *Balkenkreuz* on both sides of the fuselage, as does the badge of JG 53. The W.Nr of this machine appears to have been over-painted, there being no evidence of it on the reference photograph. *Werke Nummeren* were presented in various styles on desert aircraft and many detail differences can be noted.

BELOW: Messerschmitt Bf109G-14/Trop of I/JG 53 flown by *Hptm*. Jurgen Harder, Italy 1944. A finish that shows how fighter markings had come full circle by 1944, deliveries from the factories being in grey 74/75 splinter pattern on the top surfaces of wings and fuselage, with 76 lower surfaces. The double chevron of a *Gruppenkommandeur* appeared on both sides of the fuselage and the badge of JG 53 was presented on both sides of the nose. Shown with two 20mm cannon in underwing gondolas, this aircraft retains its factory radio call-sign, 'BS + NA'. Such markings were not uncommon on German fighters in Italy at this time.

OPPOSITE TOP: A selection of insignia and markings: (A) A variation on JG 27's badge was a 'pig over Africa' device used by 5 *Staffel*/JG 27. (B) An unusual marking noted on a Bf109F of a *Staffel* of III *Gruppe*/JG 27. (C) The wolf's head insignia of III/JG 77. (D) A black hand device was carried by aircraft of 8 *Staffel*/JG 27, a marking introduced by the *Staffelkapitän* Wolf Ettel in June 1943. (E) The black top hat of 2 *Staffel*/JG 77 was positioned behind the fuselage *Balkenkreuz* on Bf109s and carried by a number of machines in the Mediterranean. (F) Almost as well known as the 'lion over Africa' was the 'Berlin bear' of II/JG 27. The emblem dated from the time the *Gruppe* was stationed at Döberitz to protect the German capital for a period in early 1940. The bear was, of course, the device on the city's coat of arms.

OPPOSITE BOTTOM: A Volkswagen Type '82' light car used by Hans-Joachim Marseille as a personal transport in the desert and decorated with a number of reptilian and bird devices.

MESSERSCHMITT Bf109G-14/Trop of I/JG 53, 1944

A   B   C

D   E   F

VOLKSWAGEN Type '82' light car

Hauptmann pilot in regulation Luftwaffe tropical tunic and trousers, with white-topped hot-weather version of peaked cap. Knight's Cross is worn at throat under buttoned shirt collar; Iron Cross 2nd Class ribbon in buttonhole; and Iron Cross 1st Class on left breast, with pilot/observer's qualification badge. 'AFRIKA' cuff-title of Luftwaffe issue was not often seen, although photos confirm issue; army version was often worn. Rank epaulettes have yellow underlay of flying branch.

Unteroffizier pilot in tropical issue shirt and shorts, with desert 'sneakers' of Army issue. Ranking epaulettes were the only insignia officially allowed on the shirt, but breast eagles were often worn—note triangular backing of tropical version. He carries a life jacket under his arm. Light sandy drill clothing was Luftwaffe issue, while frequently used army issue was faded olive.

A deadly new opponent! A *Staffelkapitän* demonstrates to his pilots attacking techniques for intercepting the American four-engined heavy bombers, which were first met in force by day in the Mediterranean area. The wire projections on the model of the B-24 show the fields of fire of the defensive guns.

outnumbered: for instance on 26 February the Messerschmitt pilots were able to claim another 13 Kittyhawks shot down during a big battle over their own airfield, for the loss of 3 pilots. Five of the victories went to Bär, while 4 were credited to a young pilot in the more recently arrived II *Gruppe*, *Ltn.* Ernst-Wilhelm Reinert, who had claimed 104 victories in Russia and was now beginning to run close to Bär. First scoring in January, Reinert had claimed frequently over Tunisia. His best day came on 13 March, as JG 77 tried to fight a war on two fronts. In the morning his *Staffel* shot down four US P-40s over the Mareth area, and in the afternoon a whole formation of seven P-39 Airacobras was accounted for to the north, in the Thelepte area. Reinert was credited with one of the former and five of the latter.

March 1943 was to see 8th Army launch its offensive against the Mareth Line in the south, and subsequently outflank the defences at El Hamma. This was really the start of the last act in Africa; it also saw more hard air fighting all over the country as most areas came within range of units from either end. March also marked the appearance over the front of small numbers of the deadly Spitfire IX—an aircraft which did much to reverse the 'one-for-one' superiority which the Luftwaffe had so far enjoyed.

A great blow to JG 77 was inflicted on 23 March when the *Kommodore*, *Maj.* Müncheberg, went out on an early morning sortie with his wingman, seeking 'something to shoot down'. Müncheberg attacked an unsuspecting formation of US Spitfires, shooting down his 135th victim, but collided with (or was rammed by) the stricken aircraft and crashed to his death. Two days later over northern Tunisia, *Ltn.* Hans Möller, *Staffelkapitän* of I/JG 53 and victor of some 30 combats, was also shot down—apparently by one of the new Spitfire IXs flown by RAF ace Sqn. Ldr. Colin Gray. He baled out and became a prisoner. Müncheberg's place was taken by *Maj.* Johannes Steinhoff, who arrived from II/JG 52 in Russia. Recipient of the *Ritterkreuz mit Eichenlaub*, 'Macki' Steinhoff had recently claimed his 150th victory, having been involved in combat almost constantly since December 1939.

Even as the Spitfire IXs began to appear in Africa, II/JG 2 was withdrawn to France in mid-March, leaving the fighting in the hands of the Messerschmitt pilots. The *Gruppe* had achieved a tremendous success during its relatively brief stay, claiming some 150 victories for the loss of 18 Fw190s, only 8 of which fell in combat. It had also produced several of the top scorers of the campaign, including *Oblt.* Kurt Bühligen with 40, *Ltn.* Erich Rudorffer with 27 (including 8 on 9 February and 7 on the 15th), *Oblt.* Adolf Dickfeld with 18 and *Obfw.* Kurt Goltsch with 14.

Meanwhile II/JG 27 returned to action after being rested and re-equipped, joining III/JG 53 in Sicily to counter the growing appearances over the island of Malta-based Spitfires and US bomber formations from Africa. The unit was also tasked to escort transport aircraft and sea convoys to Tunis and Bizerta. Because of the growing Allied naval blockade, it was now becoming necessary to provide vital fuel and ammunition to a much greater degree by air, and a massive fleet of German and Italian transports had been assembled in Sicily. During April Allied fighters hunted these aircraft daily, on several occasions intercepting formations and inflicting devastating casualties. The Axis fighters were available in too little strength to seriously affect the issue, but they were able to take some toll of the marauding Lightnings and Kittyhawks which were doing the execution. The *Zerstörergruppen* were much involved in this work, being reinforced by the end of the month by II/ZG 1 from Russia, with more Bf110s. Their losses were heavy, but they did enjoy the occasional success. On 11 April for instance *Ltn.* Paul Bley of III/ZG 26, who had been shot down into the sea by P-38s on the 8th, was able to claim four of these fighters shot down while escorting a Ju52/3m formation. The *Gruppe* claimed a total of seven in this fight, although records show that the actual USAAF loss was three P-38s.

Over Tunisia vastly strengthened Allied air power began a great pre-offensive softening-up programme in mid-April, as all remaining Axis forces in Africa retreated into the north-eastern corner of Tunisia. Large numbers of Spitfires flew regular air superiority sweeps, which steadily whittled down the remaining Axis fighter strength. All units other than fighters were progressively withdrawn to Sicily and Italy, while on 20 April II/JG 51 followed suit. Even as it began the flight to Sicily, Spitfires engaged, and in a last fight, two more of the unit's Messerschmitts went down. On that same date I/JG 53's *Hptm.* Wolfgang Tonne, after shooting down two American Spitfires to raise his total to 122—21 of them over Tunisia—was himself killed when he crashed while landing at Bizerta.

Before the end of April, *Stab* plus I and II/JG 53 had also withdrawn to Sicily, from where they continued to fly daily sorties over the area of Tunisia still in Axis hands, often landing at airstrips there to rearm and refuel. II/JG 51 however, was withdrawn to re-equip, before being posted to Sardinia, which was coming under increasing Allied air attack. Over Tunisia the *Gruppe* had claimed about 120 victories, but had lost 33 Bf109s, 26 of them in combat—a high rate of attrition for a single *Gruppe*. Hafner had remained the unit's top scorer, but *Obfw.* Otto Schultz (not to be confused with Otto Schulz, who had served with II/JG 27 in 1942) was close behind with 18, and the *Kommandeur*, Hartmann Grasser, had claimed 11. At least six other pilots had achieved scores of five or more, including Herbert Puschmann and Karl Rammelt.

The final Allied offensive began on 22 April, the Axis front soon crumbling before it. JG 77 did what it could from bases on the Cap Bon peninsula, while the units in Sicily continued to give a hand. On 29 April one of II/JG 27's most promising pilots, *Ltn.*

'Cushioned success.' A cheerful *Jagdflieger* relaxes in the Mediterranean sun, bolstered by booty from a shot-down USAAF bomber.

Bernd Schneider, who had recently added 8 victories to the 12 he had gained over the Western Desert, shot down a P-38 for his 23rd and final victory. His own aircraft fell into the Mediterranean seconds later, victim of another of the Lightnings.

During the afternoon of 7 May 1943 both Tunis and Bizerta fell to the Allies; the remnants of the Luftwaffe were ordered to evacuate, and during the next twenty-four hours JG 77's surviving Bf109s were flown across to Sicily, each carrying two of the unit's ground personnel. During one such flight *Ltn.* Reinert, watched by his fascinated, if very cramped, passengers, came up behind a formation of Allied fighters and shot one down—his 51st victory of the campaign. Despite the efforts of the pilots, a large part of JG 77's ground echelon went into captivity with the thousands of other German and Italian troops whom it had proved impossible to evacuate. The final surrender in Africa took place on 13 May.

* * *

JG 77 had performed particularly well in Africa, claiming some 350 victories from 1 January to 8 May 1943; 68 aircraft were lost in the air, 58 of them in combat, but many more were destroyed on the ground. Reinert was top scorer in this period, but to Heinz Bär's 39 since January must be added 22 in the last two months of 1942 over Libya. *Leutnant* Heinz-Edgar Berres, *Adjutant* of I/JG 77, had claimed 26 during this same period, while up to his death, Müncheberg's total since his return to Africa had been 19. II *Gruppe's Hptm.* Anton Hackl had claimed 14, while Freytag and Ubben had also done well. Bär had been shot down on one occasion late in the campaign, and while unhurt, he had suffered a severe psychological blow to his confidence. Tired and ill, he was eventually posted home to Germany.

JG 53 was still fully operational, having claimed 239 victories since the initial operations in Tunisia. Losses had been fairly heavy, totalling 78 pilots, 52 of them in combat. The top scorer in the campaign for this *Geschwader* had been *Oblt.* Franz Schiess, now commanding a *Staffel* in III *Gruppe*; he had claimed 23. Tonne with 21 and Crinius with 14 had both been lost, but 'Tutti' Müller had added at least 11 to his total, while Fritz Dinger, Jürgen Harder, Hans Röhrig, Günther Seeger, Gerhard Michalski, Herbert Rollwage, Franz Götz, Julius Meimberg, and von Maltzahn himself had all done well.

Bf109G gains what shade and camouflage it can from the sparse foliage of a Sicilian tree.

FINALE IN ITALY

With the end of the fighting in North Africa, attention now focused on the northern side of the Mediterranean; the Allies had already prepared their plans for an invasion of Sicily, following an aerial neutralization of the fortress island of Pantelleria, situated between Africa and the Italian mainland. Throughout June, regular air attacks on this target and on airfields and defences in Sicily and southern Italy brought frequent combats as the Axis struggled to prepare themselves. II/JG 27 played an important part in the defence of Sicily and Pantelleria at this time. Between 18 and 31 May, twenty-five victories were claimed by the unit to add to the forty-eight it had achieved over Tunisia. Eight more followed over Pantelleria during early June, where the total German fighter claims reached only twenty before the island fell. The *Gruppe* suffered a severe setback however when on 10 June, a day of many combats, nine pilots were lost to US fighters.

Unsure where the next blow would fall, the Axis were forced to retain a major defence in both Sicily and Sardinia. On the latter island, the Bf109s of II/JG 51 were regularly in action against American bombers and their escorts, aided by a quite substantial Italian fighter force and a few Fw190 *Jabo*. The main Luftwaffe fighter strength was located in Sicily however, where II/JG 27 and *Stab*,

On a Sardinian airfield Axis air force personnel watch an Italian Macchi C.202 fighter come in to land. In the foreground is a Bf109G-6 of either II/JG 51 or III/JG 77, heavily armed with additional underwing 20mm cannon for anti-bomber work.

I, II and III/JG 53, were joined by various elements of II and III/ZG 1, and a number of newly arrived *Schlachtgruppen*, equipped with Fw190s. In Crete III/JG 27 was gradually being rebuilt with new equipment, while in Greece a new *Gruppe*, IV/JG 27, was in the course of formation. III/ZG 26 had been moved north to the Rome area to join Italian units in the defence of the Holy City. There the outclassed *Zerstörer* enjoyed a much greater possibility of survival and success against US bombers and their still relatively small numbers of P-38 escorts.

After its terrible ordeal in Tunisia, JG 77 was not yet operational, and was resting in southern Italy. Before the end of June it was to be thrust back into the fray, *Stab* plus I and II *Gruppen* moving to Sicily without ground crews, whilst III *Gruppe* joined II/JG 51 in Sardinia. During July the *Jagdflieger* were to be reinforced by the arrival in the Foggia area of a newly formed *Gruppe*, IV/JG 3. Commanded by *Hptm*. Franz Beyer, a *Ritterkreuzträger* who had served with other units of JG 3 in Russia and who had gained some seventy victories to date, this unit was also equipped with Bf109Gs.

The inability of the Luftwaffe to achieve much success against the US heavy bombers led to the despatch of *Inspekteur der Jagdflieger, Generalmajor* Adolf Galland, to take over the direction of the air defences in the hope of inflicting a really crushing defeat on the Allied air forces before an invasion of Sicily could be attempted. Early on 25 June III/JG 77 flew over to Trapani airfield, Sicily, from Sardinia, joining I and II/JG 77 and one *Gruppe* from JG 53. A low-level raid by B-26s, coinciding with a high altitude attack by B-17s, confused the defences however, and the results were most disappointing, only one bomber being shot down by the JG 77 *Kommodore, Maj*. Steinhoff. III/JG 77 was ordered back to Sardinia and that night a most unfair and demoralizing signal arrived from Berlin:

'To the *Jagdführer Sicilien*. During the defensive action against the bombing attack on the Straits of Messina the fighter element failed in its task. One pilot from each of the *Jagdgruppen* taking part will be tried by court-martial for cowardice in the face of the enemy. Göring, *Reichsmarshal*.'

In the event, no such court-martial took place, but the effect on the morale of the *Jagdflieger* was severe.

During early July the raids on Sicily reached a crescendo, with formation after formation of light, medium and heavy bombers, all with substantial fighter escorts, appearing over the island throughout each day. The German and Italian fighters responded, and some pitched battles were fought. On 2 July II/JG 27 was able to claim four B-24 Liberators from a big formation over Lecce, while on the 5th, I/JG 77 claimed five P-40s and II/JG 77 shot down a number of B-17s and the first photo-reconnaissance Mosquito to be lost in the area. These sorties were costly on occasion, JG 53 losing two more of its leading pilots. *Leutnant* Herbert Broennle of I *Gruppe* (57 victories), who had recently joined the unit from Russia, was killed on the 4th, and *Oblt*. Hans Röhrig of III *Gruppe* (75 victories) on the 7th.

The Allied invasion of Sicily began early on 10 July 1943. Without an adequate warning system, with their airfields already battered by constant bombing, outnumbered and on the run, the *Jagdflieger* could do little. The units in Sardinia were called upon, and the 39 Bf109s of II/JG 51 were flown to Trapani at once to join *Stab* and II/JG 27 and II/JG 77. On the first morning of the invasion all units were committed, *Stab* and I/JG 77 claiming six bombers, but losing four fighters including that flown by the *Gruppenkommandeur*. Two days later III/JG 77 arrived from Sardinia to take up station at Gerbini to protect the vital Straits of Messina—the lifeline to Italy. Heavy bombing raids rendered the airfield unusable however, and the *Gruppe* returned again to Sardinia. Other *Jagdgruppen* were being forced from the main airfields to rough strips by the constant bombing, and by the 13th, all units bar II/JG 51 had been withdrawn from western Sicily to the north-east corner of the island. Ultimately they were sent across into southern Italy, to Reggio Calabria, and the multiplicity of airfields on the Foggia plain.

Meanwhile III/ZG 26 was ordered back to the island from Rome, and was thrown into action in the ground attack rôle. Severe casualties were suffered both to fighters and ground fire, and the unit was soon withdrawn again, together with the other *Zerstörergruppen*.

In such circumstances victories were not easy to come by, most pilots being more than occupied in fighting desperately for their own survival against the ever-present hordes of Allied fighters. Some pilots, such as Reinert and Werner Schroer, still managed to achieve results, but they were the exception rather than the rule. On 15 July 8/JG 27 was sent from Crete to Brindisi in southern Italy as a reinforcement. The *Staffel* was now led by *Oblt.* Wolf Ettel, an ex-JG 3 *Ritterkreuzträger* from the Russian front with 120 victories to his credit. In three days the unit claimed five victories, all but one credited to Ettel. On the 16th, the *Staffel* joined with II/JG 27 in an interception of B-24s, and again good results were claimed, nine of the big bombers being reported shot down, two each by Ettel and Schroer. Next day however, 8 *Staffel* lost four pilots killed, Ettel included.

By that time, II/JG 51 had only four Bf109s left serviceable, and was withdrawn to southern Italy, most of its aircraft having been destroyed or damaged on the ground by bombing. With surface craft in the Straits of Messina under constant air attack, efforts were made to partially resupply the forces still fighting around the Messina area by air. On 25 July Bf109s of I/JG 77 and II/JG 27 attempted to protect a formation of Ju52/3ms from slaughter by Spitfires of No. 322 Wing, RAF. They were overwhelmed, and amongst those lost was *Oblt.* Heinz-Edgar Berres of I/JG 77. This *Ritterkreuzträger* had by then increased his score to 53, all but 6 of them in the Mediterranean area. Two

Bf109G-6 of II/JG 51 on a Sardinian airfield, summer 1943.

days later II/JG 53's *Oblt.* Fritz Dinger (67 victories) was killed on the ground by bomb fragments during a raid on his own airfield.

With Germany itself now coming under heavy bombing attack, home defence was becoming a priority. Following its notable successes against the US 'heavies', II/JG 27 was ordered from Italy to Reich defence duties on 28 July, handing its remaining Bf109s to the *Gruppen* of JG 3, 53, and 77 at Foggia. Since the end of the Tunisian campaign the unit had claimed 73 more victories, including 35 four-engined bombers. *Hauptmann* Werner Schroer (now the *Kommandeur*) had claimed 15 during this period to raise his Mediterranean score to 85. Top scorer during this phase had been *Ltn.* Willi Kientsch with 18, bringing his personal total to 41, while *Hptm.* Ernst Börngen had claimed 9 to raise his score to 28 and *Fw.* Heinrich Steis 6, to reach 20.

II/JG 51 also withdrew to the Reich for re-equipment, while *Stab*/ZG 2, III/ZG 1, and III/ZG 26 went home to form the nucleus of a new home-defence *Zerstörergeschwader* 26. II/ZG 1 took its remaining Bf110s to Brest in France for patrols over the Bay of Biscay against RAF anti-submarine aircraft.

Even as the fighting in Sicily raged, a large force of B-24s from Africa flew unescorted across the Mediterranean on 1 August, making for the oil refineries at Ploesti in Rumania. The bombers were attacked en route by aircraft of IV/JG 27 from Greece, and by elements of the defending I/JG 4 at the target. Losses were substantial, fifty-one bombers failing to return. At least ten of these are known to have been shot down by German fighters, over half of them falling to the Greek-based aircraft—IV *Gruppe* had enjoyed an auspicious baptism of fire.

Italy was by now almost a lost cause so far as the Luftwaffe was concerned, the calls of other fronts—and particularly the increasingly critical defence of the homeland—being given prior consideration. While the main fighter forces had been locked in battle over Sicily during July, the US heavy bombers had made a number of raids on southern and central Italy, meeting only limited resistance. The withdrawal of many Luftwaffe units to this area during August changed this pattern by the end of that month however. On 25 August 140 P-38s staged a strafing attack on the Foggia complex, during which a large number of Axis aircraft—mainly bombers—were destroyed on the ground without the *Jagdflieger* having the opportunity to offer any worthwhile resistance. Such was not the case on the 30th: a B-25 raid on Aversa marshalling yards was intercepted by a big force of Bf109s, which succeeded in shooting down thirteen of the escorting P-38s, although none of the bombers were brought down.

No opposition could be offered to the initial Allied landings on the 'toe' of Italy on 1 September, but next day the Luftwaffe again rose in strength to battle with American bombers and their escorts attacking Cancello marshalling yards near Naples. This time ten P-38s were shot down, but German

A II/JG 51 Bf109G-6 comes in to land in Sardinia. Note *Regia Aeronautica* Savoia SM82 transport on right.

losses were also heavy, including *Oblt.* Franz Schiess of III/JG 53 (67 victories), one of the top scorers of the Tunisian campaign, who was shot down into the Mediterranean and never seen again.

This was to be the last large-scale resistance offered to the bomber formations for some weeks, for a new crisis was about to develop. Just before a very dangerous large-scale landing by Anglo-American troops of US 5th Army could go ashore on 9 September the Italian government requested an armistice and ceased fighting. Operating alone now, the Luftwaffe made frequent small-scale raids on the Allied beach-head and offshore shipping in the Salerno area, the fighters escorting *Schlachtflieger* strikes made from Foggia. These achieved little more than nuisance effect, and attrition was high. Before the month was out Foggia had been evacuated due to the advance of 8th Army troops from the south, who were moving up the east coast, and to another day of severe strafing attacks by US P-38s. Airfields around Rome then became the main base for operations in support of the ground forces, while part of the available strength was moved further north to protect the industrial areas from the growing weight of heavy bomber attacks.

Following the move northwards from Foggia, IV/JG 3 withdrew to join the rest of the *Geschwader* on Reich defence. At the same time the German garrison was withdrawn from Sardinia, it being

realized that this island had become indefensible. The Luftwaffe units involved moved to the Rome area, substantially reinforcing the units arriving there from Foggia. III/JG 77 was one of those coming from Sardinia, having also operated briefly from airfields in Corsica, but in October this unit was despatched to Mizil in Rumania, to join the defences against the increasing threat of bomber attacks being renewed against the Ploesti targets. In November, II/JG 53 was withdrawn to Vienna for home defence, since the first raids by US heavy bombers, now newly moved to the Foggia area, had been made on targets in Austria during the previous month. These departures were made good at the end of 1943 by the return of II/JG 51, which had re-equipped following its Sicilian debacle, and by the arrival in northern Italy of I/JG 4 from Rumania. This latter unit was commanded by *Hptm.* Hans 'Gockel' (gamecock) Hahn, a pilot with some twenty victories to his credit. One of the *Gruppe*'s leading pilots was *Oblt.* Wilhelm Steinmann, *Staffelkapitän* of 1 *Staffel*.

Meanwhile during October 1943, *Obstlt.* Günther von Maltzahn, *Kommodore* of JG 53, had been promoted to the post of *Jagdführer Italien*. His place at the head of the *'Pik As' Geschwader* was taken by *Maj.* Helmut Bennemann, a veteran fighter pilot from the Eastern Front with a *Ritterkreuz* and over seventy victories. He was to be ably aided by the

Bf109G-6s of II/JG 51 in Sardinia, 1943.

redoubtable 'Tutti' Müller, who now became deputy *Kommodore*.

Late in January 1944 a further Allied landing was made on the west coast at Anzio, designed to speed the fall of the German defences around Monte Cassino and the consequent capture of Rome. Although the Luftwaffe could in no way match the level of air support provided by the Allies at this time, no effort was spared with what was available to attack the Allied beach-head, and to support the harassed ground forces as much as possible. Attrition was again high however, and was not eased by two major contributory factors. In

November 1943 the US 15th Air Force had been formed to undertake strategic bombing attacks on targets in southern Europe, and initially many of these were directed at northern Italian locations. By mid-December improved escort fighters were appearing in the shape of P-47 Thunderbolts, and a proportion of the *Jagdgruppen* were tied down in the north at airfields such as Udine and Villaorba, joined by units of the new *Republica Sociale Italiana* air force, to provide some measure of protection. At the end of January 1944 in support of the Anzio operations, these 15th Air Force units undertook a series of damaging attacks on the northern Italian airfields. At the same time Allied fighters based on Corsica, which was now in Franco-American hands, were starting to make offensive sweeps over the areas directly to the north of Rome.

This multiplicity of problems caused a diversion of effort, with the units of JG 77 tending to concentrate on air defence, while I/JG 4, II/JG 51, plus I and III/JG 53 were thrown into the fighting over Anzio and Cassino, escorting *Schlacht* aircraft and attacking Allied fighter-bombers and bomber formations. Allied fighter patrols were everywhere however, and I/JG 4 for instance lost fourteen pilots killed, wounded or taken prisoner during the first six weeks of 1944, including the *Kommandeur*, 'Gockel' Hahn, who fell on 27 January. II/JG 51 also

suffered heavily, losing one of its leading lights, *Ritterkreuzträger Hptm.* Herbert Puschmann (54 victories) in combat with medium bombers on 3 February. This month saw the final reinforcement of the Italian front with the arrival of I/JG 2 from France—the first Fw190 *Jagdgruppe* (as opposed to *Schlachtgruppe*) to see action in the area since the fighting over Tunisia a year earlier. The unit was commanded by *Hptm.* Franz Hrdlicka, an ex-JG 77 pilot who had taken part in that earlier campaign, 1 *Staffel* was led by *Oblt.* Siegfried 'Wumm' Lemke, who had just received his *Ritterkreuz* after his 47th victory.

Activity both over the front and against the growing formations of heavy bombers and their escorts continued during early 1944. On one occasion at the start of March the *Jagdflieger* enjoyed one welcome success when they were able to claim nine P-47s shot down in a single combat. By then however the 15th Air Force was sending an increasing number of its raids over Bulgaria, Hungary and Rumania, such attacks being directed north-east from Foggia, missing the units based in Italy. In April the first P-51 Mustangs appeared with the bombers, but raids on Italian targets were much fewer. Attacks on German and Austrian locations nevertheless required an overflight of the area, and on such occasions the German and Italian interceptors were up to meet them as they passed, both going out and coming back.

A Bf109G-6 of II/JG 51 taxis out for a sortie.

In April I/JG 2 returned to France, while II/JG 51 also withdrew again, this time moving to Nish in Yugoslavia to join in the defence against the bombers heading for Rumania and Hungary. It remained there during the spring and summer of 1944, coming under the control of *Luftflotte* 1 (see *Luftwaffe Fighter Units, Russia, 1941–45* for further details of the later operations of this unit). JG 77 was at this time losing a number of its leading *Experten*, though not all in combat. *Hauptmann* Anton Hackl, *Gruppenkommandeur* of II *Gruppe*, left to take over III/JG 11 in Germany during autumn 1943, while III *Gruppe*'s leader, Kurt Ubben, was posted from Rumania to command JG 2 in France in March 1944. His successor, *Hptm.* Emil Omert, was shot down and killed on 24 April 1944 while attempting to intercept a bomber formation over Ploesti; he had claimed some seventy victories on all fronts before his death. The following month the withdrawal of the remaining *Gruppen* of JG 53 began.

The position of the German fighters in Italy was now practically hopeless, as they were so heavily outnumbered and with no prospect of further

Sicilian defender. Bf109Gs of II/JG 27 were very active in the defence of Sicily against US heavy bomber attacks during the summer of 1943. Here ground crew push one of these aircraft (fitted with underwing cannon) into a dispersal in an olive grove.

reinforcement. When the Allied spring offensive of 1944 began in May, breaking through the Gustav Line defences and linking up with the Anzio beach-head, only JG 77 and I/JG 4 remained in Italy. On 5 June Rome fell, and next day Normandy was invaded. Faced with this invasion in the west, and an imminent and massive Russian offensive in the east, Italy diminished still further on the Luftwaffe priority list, and before the end of June JG 77 had been withdrawn to join the fray in France, followed shortly after by I/JG 4, which went to home defence. The further defence of the area south of the Alps was left to the Italian Fascist air force. .

Throughout this period there had been one brighter spot for the Luftwaffe, namely the performance of the fighter units in the Balkans and Aegean area. As already mentioned, IV/JG 27 had entered combat over western Greece and the Adriatic Sea during mid-summer 1943, while III/JG 27 had also

In spring 1943, II/ZG 1 arrived in Sicily to aid in the late stages of the Tunisian campaign. The *Gruppe* had been withdrawn by the end of July, but several unserviceable aircraft were subsequently captured by the Allies in Sicily and southern Italy. One of these casualties of war is seen here with the *Wespen* emblem on the nose; in the foreground several upper nose cowlings can be seen, at least three of which carry segments of this colourful marking. (IWM)

become fully operational again shortly afterwards, setting up detachments in southern Greece, and on the islands of Crete and Rhodes.

During September 1943 the British launched a risky and ill-conceived invasion of the Aegean islands of Kos, Leros and Samsos, flying in a squadron of Spitfires to the only available airfield, located on Kos. The Germans countered with an immediate series of air attacks in the middle of the month, escorted by aircraft of IV/JG 27, which shot down several of the defending Spitfires. A week later a counter-invasion was mounted, support this time coming from III *Gruppe*. The British defences, both air and ground, were swiftly overwhelmed, this unit also enjoying some combat successes.

To support the British, the Americans made a number of heavy bomber attacks on airfields in Greece, and during the autumn both *Gruppen* of JG 27 were heavily involved against the US formations, claiming a heavy toll of them. In three months IV

Gruppe claimed 55 victories, including 31 against P-38 fighters. Its best day occurred on 15 November, when 14 victories were claimed, 13 of them against Lightnings. The *Kommandeur*, *Oblt*. Joachim Kirschner, had arrived to take command of the *Gruppe* on its formation, having already claimed 173 victories on the Russian front and two over Malta with II/JG 3 during early 1942. In less than four weeks Kirschner added 13 more over the Balkans, but was then shot down by Spitfires of No. 1435 Squadron, RAF, over Yugoslavia. He managed to bale out, but was captured by partisans, who shot him.

Oberfeldwebel Heinrich Bartels had claimed 47 victories in Russia before joining IV/JG 27. He was to be the unit's most successful pilot in the Mediterranean area, claiming 21 further successes during October and November. Losses were heavy however, and by the end of 1943 when the *Gruppe* was withdrawn to Germany for home defence duties, it had suffered the loss of 21 pilots in three months. It must be said that IV/JG 27 seems to have been rather optimistic in its claiming, the numbers of P-38s and US bombers listed in the unit's totals having proved much more difficult to substantiate from records than has been the case with some of the other units involved in the fighting at this time, including III/JG 27. This latter *Gruppe*'s various detachments were regularly in action during this period, both against heavy bomber raids, and against RAF Beaufighters and medium bombers which attempted to stop the supply shipping which was provisioning the garrisons of the Aegean islands. Successes were frequent, but attrition was also quite severe, particularly when attacking the well-defended American formations. Between September 1943 and March 1944 the *Gruppe* was to claim 97 victories, 19 of them four-engined bombers and 32 Beaufighters; losses during this time totalled 24 pilots killed, wounded or missing. The *Gruppenkommandeur*, Ernst Düllberg, claimed 10 of the victories to add to 10 which he had gained with II *Gruppe* in Africa during 1942. *Leutnant* Fritz Gromotka claimed 9 to bring his Mediterranean total to 13, while *Ltn*. Hans-Gunnar Culemann claimed 7.

During late 1943 and the first half of 1944, JG 77 played a major part in the air defence of northern Italy. Here a newly delivered Bf109G-14 of II *Gruppe* carries the *Geschwader*'s new marking—instituted in honour of the late *Kommodore, Maj.* Müncheberg, whose personal emblem had been a red heart.

During March 1944 III/JG 27 also began withdrawing to the Reich, but a small detachment was left for the defence of Crete, which was now under regular attack by RAF units based in Egypt. A considerable success was gained on 6 March when the Bf109s intercepted an unescorted formation of South African Marauders. Five of the bombers were claimed shot down although four actually failed to return. Such raids then ceased until May 1944, when the RAF was at last able to introduce effective escorts in the shape of Spitfire IXs and Mustang IIIs. These aircraft swiftly reduced the effectiveness of the German detachment which, following several losses, had ceased to operate by the end of June.

Thereafter German fighter activity in the Mediterranean area was limited to occasional sorties over the Balkans and the Alps by units operating with *Luftflotte* 1 on the southern sector of the Eastern Front.

JAGD- and ZERSTÖRER Units, Mediterranean Area, 1941–44

I/JG 2	Italy, February–April 1944
II/JG 2	Tunisia, November 1942–March 1943
11/JG 2	Sicily, November 1942, incorporated into II/JG 53
II/JG 3	Sicily, December 1941–May 1942 (6 *Staffel* detached North Africa, April 1942)
IV/JG 3	Southern Italy, July–September 1943
I/JG 4	Northern Italy, December 1943–July 1944
7/JG 26	Sicily, February–May 1941 / North Africa, May–July 1941
11/JG 26	Tunisia, November 1942, incorporated into II/JG 51
I/JG 27	Yugoslav invasion, April 1941 / North Africa, April 1941–November 1942 / Sicily, October 1942
II/JG 27	Yugoslavia and Greece, April 1941 / North Africa, September 1941–December 1942 / Sicily and southern Italy, March–July 1943
III/JG 27	Yugoslavia and Greece, April 1941 / Sicily, May 1941 / North Africa, December 1941–November 1942 / Greece and Crete, November 1942–June 1944 (8 *Staffel* detached Italy July 1943)
IV/JG 27	Balkans, August–December 1943
II/JG 51	Tunisia, November 1942–April 1943 / Sardinia and Sicily, June–July 1943 / Northern Italy, December 1943–February 1944
III/JG 52	Yugoslavia and Crete, April–May 1941 (Reserve only)
I/JG 53	Sicily, December 1941–May 1942 / Sicily, Tunisia, Italy, October 1942–May 1944
II/JG 53	Sicily, Tunisia, Italy, December 1941–November 1943
III/JG 53	Sicily, North Africa, Tunisia, Italy, December 1941–May 1944
II/JG 54	Yugoslav invasion, April 1941
III/JG 54	Yugoslav invasion, April 1941

I/JG 77 (previously I(J)/LG 2)	Yugoslavia, Greece, Crete, April–May 1941 / Sicily, North Africa, Tunisia, Italy, July 1942–June 1944 / Yugoslavia, Greece, Crete, April–May 1941
II/JG 77	North Africa, Tunisia, Sicily, Italy, December 1942–June 1944
III/JG 77	Yugoslavia, Greece and Crete, April–May 1941 / North Africa, Tunisia, October 1942–May 1943 / Sardinia, Sicily, Corsica, Italy, June–October 1943 / Rumania, October 1943–June 1944
II/ZG 1	Sicily, Italy, April–July 1943

Jabogruppe Afrika

10 (*Jabo*)/JG 27	North Africa, late 1941–October 1942	October 1942, together formed I/Sch.G 2 and new III/ZG 1
10 (*Jabo*)/JG 53	Sicily, North Africa, December 1941–October 1942	
III/ZG 1	North Africa, August–October 1942	

III/ZG 1 (new)	Sicily, November 1942–July 1943
III/ZG 2 (part)	Tunisia, November 1942–February 1943 (Redesignated III/SKG 10 in February 1943)
I/ZG 26	Yugoslavia, Greece and Crete, April–May 1941 (2 *Staffel* detached North Africa, Jan.–Feb. 1941)
II/ZG 26	Yugoslavia, Greece and Crete, April–May 1941
III/ZG 26	Sicily, North Africa, Crete, Italy, January 1941–July 1943
10/ZG 26	North Africa, Crete, Sicily, Italy, mid-1942–July 1943
II/ZG 76 (less 4 *Staffel*)	Crete, May 1941
4/ZG 76	Iraq, May 1941
12/LG 1	North Africa, Crete, April 1942–? (believed to have been incorporated into 10/ZG 26 in mid-1942)

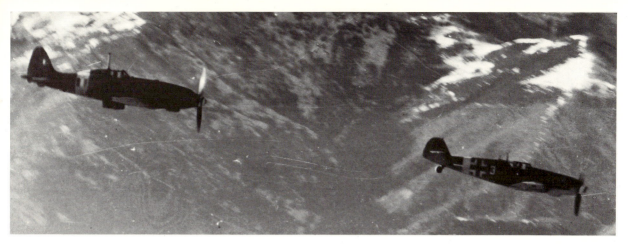

Over the mountains of northern Italy a Macchi C.205 fighter of the new RSI air force accompanies a Bf109G of II/JG 77.

The *Gruppenkommandeur* of I/JG 53 during early 1944 was *Hptm.* Jürgen Harder, seen here with his Bf109G on an Italian airfield. Note the fairing in the foreground which has been removed from the underwing cannon; the weapon itself has been taken out for cleaning.

SELECTED BIBLIOGRAPHY

Die Ritterkreuzträger der Luftwaffe, 1939–1945; Band 1, Jagdflieger; Ernst Obermaier; Verlag Dieter Hoffmann, 1966.

Die Verbände der Luftwaffe, 1935–1945; Wolfgang Dierich; Motorbuch Verlag, 1976.

Jagdgeschwader 27; Werner Girbig and Hans Ring; Motorbuch Verlag, 1971.

Fighters Over the Desert; Christopher Shores and Hans Ring; Neville Spearman, 1969.

Fighters Over Tunisia; Christopher Shores, Hans Ring and William Hess; Neville Spearman, 1975.

Mediterranean Air War, Vol. III; Christopher Shores; Ian Allan, 1974.

The Straits of Messina; Johannes Steinhoff; Andre Deutsch, 1971.

The Last Battle; Peter Henn; William Kimber, 1954.

Bf109G-6 of the recently formed IV/JG 27 in flight over the Balkans, late in 1943.

A Bf109G-6 is prepared for take-off. It is believed to be an aircraft of III/JG 27 in southern Greece, late 1943/early 1944.

The end of it all. Grave of a Luftwaffe *Jagdflieger* in North Africa. (M. Schoeman)

Notes sur les planches en couleur

Page 25: *Oberleutnant* Hans-Joachim Marseille, juin 1942, peindu d'une photographie. Il porte version des tropiques d'un calot sans tuyautage de grade d'officier; un dolman d'aviateur de cuir noir avec quatre taches personellement obtenu; et pantalon des tropiques distribués de l'armée avec bottes normales d'aviateur. Le dolman porte son insigne de la Croix d'Allemagne sur le sein droit, sa Croix de Fer 1ère Classe sur le gauche et épaulettes de grade. Couleur d'écharpe spéculative.

Page 26 dessus: Messerschmitt Bf109E-7/U2 of III/JG 27 volé de Erbo Graf von Kageneck, Balkans, printemps 1941. Premiers avions arrivés dans la région méditerranéenne portèrent camouflage normal européen pour une période de courte durée—en ce cas un dessin éclaté de gris 74 et 75 sur les hautes surfaces et 76 blanc-bleu sur les côtés des dessous. La raie blanche sur fuselage à l'arrière devint plus tard un marquage d'identification normal pour avions de chasse avec extremités d'escadres blanches, une couverture de bossage blanche et la section en avant du capotage de machine blanc. La situation du numéro individuel d'avion sur le capotage fut d'usage commun pendant cette période.

Page 26 dessous: Messerschmitt Bf109E de I/JG 27, Afrique du nord, été 1941. À moins de quelques semaines d'arrivée en pays de désert, ces fractions d'avions de bombardement destinées à rester pour une durée repeignirent leurs appareils en couleurs plus appropriées à leur nouvelle région de campagne. Cet appareil, de JG 27, tient la couleur de sable jaune 79 sur hautes surfaces et bleu 78 en bas, la première étante surpeindue avec nuance 80. Il y eut apparemment deux nuances de cette couleur avec une teinte brune ou verte et la première est illustrée ici. L'insigne du 'Lion au-dessus d'Afrique' de JG27 fut beaucoup appliqué au Bf109E.

Page 27: Messerschmitt Bf109F de I/JG 27 volé de Oberleutnant Hans-Joachim Marseille, juin 1942. Un de plusieurs Bf109s volé du pilote de chasse de Luftwaffe avec un grand compte dans le désert, le dessin dépeignit l'appareil utilisé pour marquer victoires 82 et 83 le 11 June 1942. L'appareil porte la combinaison de couleurs beaucoup utilisée de couleur de sable 79 et bleu 78 avec un marquage de division horizontal sur fuselage et pleins marquages d'identification blancs.

Pages 28–29: Messerschmitt Bf109E de III/JG 53 'Pik As' montrant la combinaison introduite au début de 1942—couleur de sable 79 totale sur les hautes surfaces et bleu 78 en bas. Le marquage de barre verticale pour indiquer III Gruppe est montré à l'arrière du Balkankreuz sur les deux côtés du fuselage, comme aussi l'insigne de JG 53.

Page 30: Messerschmitt Bf109G-14/Trop de I/JG 53 volé de *Hptm.* Harder, Italy 1944. Un fini qui montre la manière dans laquelle marquages d'avions de bombardement furent révolus pendant 1944, livraisons des fabriques étantes en dessin éclaté de gris 74/75 sur les hautes surfaces d'escadres et de fuselage avec 76 sur les plus bas surfaces. Le chevron en deux d'un *Gruppenkommodore* fut montré sur les deux côtés du fuselage et l'insigne de JG 53 fut montré sur les deux côtés du nez.

Page 31 dessus: Une sélection d'insignes et de marquages. (A) Une variation de l'insigne de JG 27 fut une devise d'un 'Cochon au-dessus d'Afrique' utilisé de 5 *Staffel*/JG 27. (B) Un marquage peu commun note sur un Bf109F d'une III *Gruppe Staffel* de JG 27. (C) Les insignes de la tête de loup de III/JG 77. (D) Une devise d'une main noire fut portée d'avions de 8 *Staffel*/JG 27, un marquage qui fut introduit du *Staffelkapitän* Wolf Ettel en juin 1943. (E) Le chapeau haut de forme noire de 2 *Staffel*/JG 77 fut placé en arrière de *Balkankreuz* de fuselage sur Bf109s et fut porté de plusieurs appareils dans la région méditerranéenne. (F) Presque aussi bien connu que le 'Lion au-dessus d'Afrique' fut 'L'Ours de Berlin' de II/JG 27.

Page 31 dessous: Une auto légère Volkswagen Type '82' utilisée de Hans-Joachim Marseille comme transport personnel dans le désert et décorée avec un certain nombre de devises de reptiles et d'oiseaux.

Page 32 gauche: *Unteroffizier* pilote mis en chemise et culotte courte de distribution tropicale, avec bottes courtes à désert de distribution d'Armée. Épaulettes de grade étaient les seuls insignes officiellement autorisés sur chemise, mais insignes d'aigles étaient souvent portés—prenez note de pièce triangulaire sur les dos de version des tropiques. Il porte une ceinture de sauvetage sur bras. Vêtements roux clairs de manoeuvre par distribution de Luftwaffe en même temps que la distribution d'Armée beaucoup utilisée fut la fondue de couleur olive.

Page 32 droit: *Hauptmann-pilot* mis en tunique et pantalons réglementaire des tropiques de Luftwaffe avec version pour temps chaud de casquette avec haute surface blanche. L'insigne de Croix de Chevalier est porté à gorge sous col de chemise boutonné; Croix de Fer 1ère Classe sur sein gauche, avec insigne de qualification de pilote/observateur au-dessous. Titre d' 'AFRIKA' sur manchette de distribution de Luftwaffe ne fut pas beaucoup vu bien que photos confirment distribution; la version d'Armée fut beaucoup portée. Épaulettes de grade tiennent sous-étoffe jaune de rameau d'aviation.

Farbtafeln

Seite 25: Oberleutnant Hans-Joachim Marseille, Juni 1942, von einer Photographie gemalt. Er trägt tropische Version Luftwaffefeldmütze ohne Offiziers-patentgradlitze; eine persönliche gekaufte Fliegerschutzjacke mit vier Taschen; und Tropenhose von der Armee ausgegeben mit Normalfliegerstiefeln. Die Jacke trägt sein Deutsches Kreuz auf seiner rechten Brust, sein Eisernes Kreuz 1ster Klasse auf der Linker und Dienstgradepauletten. Farbe der Schärpe ist erdacht.

Seite 32 links: Unteroffizierpilot in ausgegebenem Tropenhemd und ausgegebener kurzer Hose mit 'Turnschuhen' zum Tragen in der Wüste von der Armee ausgegeben. Dienstgradepauletten waren die einzige Abzeichen, die am Hemd offiziell gestatten wurden aber an der Brust wurden oft getragen—bemerken dreieckiges Stück Tropenversion. Er trägt einen Rettungsgürtel unter seinem Arm. Kleidung aus hellsandfarbigem Drillich war Luftwaffeausgabe, während der viel oft angewendeten Ausgabe der Armee verschossene Oliven-farbe war.

Seite 32 rechts: Hauptmannpilot in Kommisstropenwaffenrock und Hose der Luftwaffe mit Version für heisses Wetter der Schirmmütze mit weisser Oberfläche. Ritterkreuz wird am Hals unter zugeknöpftem Hemdkragen getragen. Ordensband Eisernes Kreuzes 2ter Klasse im Kompfloch; und eisernes Kreuz 1ster Klasse an linker Brust mit Befähigungsabzeichen Pilots/Orters. 'AFRIKA'-Titel an Stulpe Luftwaffeausgabe wurde nicht oft gesehen, obgleich Photographien Ausgabe bestätigen: Armeeversion wurde oft getragen. Dienstgradepauletten haben gelbes Unterstoff Fliegerwaffengattung.

Seite 26 oben: Messerschmitt Bf109E-7/U2 der III/JG 27, Frühling 1941, von Erbo Graf von Kageneck, Balkans, geführt. Frühe ankommende Flugzeuge in das Gebiet Mittelmeers trugen europäische Normaltarnung für eine kurze Zeit—in diesem Fall eine Splittermusterprobe grauer Farben 74 und 75 auf den Oberflächen und 76 weiss-blau auf den Unterseiten. Das weisse Hinterrumpfband wurde ein Normalkennabzeichen für Jägers zusammen mit weissen Tragflächenenden, Propellornabe und vorderem Stück Motorverkleidung. Die Stellung der Einzelnummer des Flugzeugs auf der Verkleidung auf einem kreisförmigen Hintergrund war während dieser Zeit in III/JG 27 viel angewendet.

Seite 26 unten: Messerschmitt Bf109E der I/JG 27, Sommer 1941, Nordafrika. Binnen ein paar Wochen Ankunft in Wüstehimmelstrichen bespritzten diese Jägerverbände, die für eine Zeitdauer hier in der Wüste zu bleiben sollten, ihre Flugzeuge wieder mit Anstrich in Farben, die viel mehr passend zu einem neuen Operationsgebiet wurden. Dies Flugzeug der I/JG 27 hat sandgelbe Farbe 79 auf Oberflächen und blaue Farbe 78 unter, die erste mit Farbton 80 übergespritzt wird. Es gab scheinbarlich zwei Farbtöne dieser Farbe mit entweder einer braunen oder grünen Färbung und die erste hat man hier illustriert. Das Abzeichen des 'Löwes Afrikas' der JG 27 wurde viel zu dem Bf109E angewendet.

Seite 27: Messerschmitt Bf109F der I/JG 27, Juni 1942 von Oberleutnant Hans-Joachim Marseille geführt. Ein vieler Bf109s von den Luftwaffe-Jagdfliegern mit vielen Erfolgen in der Wüste geführt zeigt dies Bild das Flugzeug, das am 11 Juni 1942 Erfolge 82 und 83 davonzutragen angewendet wurde. Das Flugzeug trägt die viel angewendete Farbenzusammenstellung Sandfarbe 79 und Blaufarbe 78 mit waagerechter Rumpftrennungslinie und ganz weissen Hoheitsabzeichen.

Seiten 28-29: Messerschmitt Bf109F der III/JG 53 'Pik As', das die Farbenzusammenstellung zeigt, die im Frühjahr 1942 eingeführt wurde—Gesamtsandfarbe 79 auf Oberflächen und Blau 78 unter. Das senkrechte Riegelabzeichen, das benutzt wurde, um III Gruppe zu bezeichnen, wird sichtbar achtern des Balkenkreuzes auf beiden Seiten des Rumpfs, wie auch das Abzeichen der JG 53.

Seite 30: Messerschmitt Bf109G-14/Trop der I/JG 53 in 1944 von Hptm. Harder in Italien geführt. Eine Oberflächengüte, die zeigt, wie Jägerhoheitsabzeichen in 1944 rund herum gekommen waren, Lieferungen von den Fabriken wurden in einer grauen Splittermusterprobe 74/75 auf den Oberflächen der Tragflächen und des Rumpfs mit 76 auf unteren Flächen. Der Doppelwinkel eines Gruppenkommodores wurde sichtbar auf beiden Seiten des Rumpfs und das Abzeichen der JG 53 wurde auf beiden Seiten der Rumpfspitze gezeigt.

Seite 31 oben: Eine Auswahl Abzeichen und Hoheitsabzeichen. (A) Eine Veränderung des Abzeichens JG 27s war ein Sinnbild eines 'Schwein Afrikas' von 5 Staffel/JG 27 angewendet. (B) Ein ungewöhnliches Abzeichen auf einem Bf109F einer III Gruppe Staffel/JG 27 bemerke. (C) Die wolfskopfabzeichen III/JG 27. (D) Ein Sinnbild einer schwarzen Hand wurde von Flugzeugen 8 Staffel/JG 27 getragen, ein Abzeichen in Juni 1943 von Staffelkapitän Wolf Ettel eingeführt. (E) Der schwarze Zylinder 2 Staffel/JG 77 wurde auf Bf109s hinter dem Balkenkreuz am Rumpf gesteckt und wurde von vielen Flugzeugen in dem Mittelmeeresgebiet getragen. (F) Fast gut bekannt als der 'Löwe Afrikas' war der 'Berline Bär' II/JG 27.

Seite 31 unten: Ein leichter Volkswagen Type '82' Wagen von Hans-Joachim Marseille als persönlichen Transport in der Wüste angewendet und mit vielen Sinnbildern Reptilien und Vögel geziert.

AIRWAR SERIES

First 20 titles: